MW00698144

REVIVAL FIRE

Discerning
Between
The True & The False

Eddie L. Hyatt

Psalm 67:1-2

A Publication of
HYATT PRESS
2009

REVIVAL FIRE: *Discerning Between the True & the False*
By Eddie L. Hyatt
© 2009 by Hyatt International Ministries, Incorporated
ALL RIGHTS RESERVED.

Published by Hyatt Press
A Subsidiary of Hyatt Int'l Ministries, Incorporated

Mailing Address (2009)
9933 S. 108th East Avenue
Tulsa, OK 76133

Internet Addresses
Email: DrEddieHyatt@gmail.com
Web Site: www.EddieHyatt.com

Unless otherwise indicated, all Scripture quotations
are taken from the New Kings James Version of the Bible.
© 1979, 1980, 1982 by Thomas Nelson, Inc. Publishers.

ISBN 978-1-888435-20-7

Library of Congress Control Number
Pending

Printed in the United States of America

CONTENTS

I cannot know God by feelings
and impressions. I can only know
God by His Word.
Smith Wigglesworth

PREFACE

Throughout church history, God has graciously blessed His people with outpourings of the Holy Spirit, *i.e.,* with *Revival Fire.* These same revivals, however, have been plagued with fleshly and false doctrines and manifestations, *i.e.,* with "strange fire." For example, during the 18th century Methodist revival, John Wesley admitted that "nature mixed with grace" and that "Satan likewise mimicked this work of God, in order to discredit the whole work."[1]

Historically, there have been two extreme responses to this state of affairs. On the one hand, many have reacted to the extremes by rejecting all revival. On the other hand, others have put their heads in the sand and refused to recognize any wrongdoing or falsehood in revival.

Neither response is reasonable or Biblical. We must take the time and make the effort to learn to discern between the true and the false. When faced with the reality of "strange fire" in the Methodist revival, Wesley expressed confidence that God, "will enable us to discern how far, in every case, the work is pure, and where it mixes and degenerates."[2]

---

[1] John Wesley, vol. 8 of *The Works of John Wesley*, 14 vols. (Grand Rapids: Zondervan, n.d.), 519.

[2] Wesley, vol. 8 of *The Works of John Wesley*, 519.

"Strange Fire" Is Offering Worship to God That is Foreign to His Revelation in Scripture.

"Strange fire" in the House of the LORD is not something new. It is older than the New Testament. Leviticus 10:1-3 tells the story of Nadab and Abihu, the two sons of Aaron, offering *profane fire* before the Lord. The Hebrew word translated "profane" in the NKJV literally means "strange" or "foreign." We are not told exactly what they did, but they obviously sought to worship God in a way that was foreign to the manner that had been prescribed by God. As a result, *fire went out from the Lord and devoured them.*

Fire Speaks of Intensity, Passion & Commitment.

Fire is used figuratively in Scripture to refer to extreme passion, enthusiasm and commitment for the things of God. It is also used in reference to the purifying effect of God on the human soul in the same way that fire has a purifying effect on precious metals, such as gold. In Scripture, God often manifests Himself in the form of fire, bringing blessing and affirmation, but also judgment, as with Nadab and Abihu.

There was much fire in the Old Testament worship of Yahweh. There were various burnt offerings that were continually offered in worship on behalf of the Israelites. In fact, Aaron was told that the fire was never to go out on the altar where the burnt offerings were daily offered to the LORD (Leviticus 6:8-13). God often showed His pleasure by sending fire and consuming the sacrifice that was being offered.

"Strange Fire" Brought Judgment.

On this particular day, Nadab and Abihu filled their censers with fire as they, no doubt, had done many times in their duties as priests in the Aaronic priesthood. This time, however, they proceeded to act in a manner, *which He had not commanded them.* In other words, they acted in a careless and reckless manner that was foreign or "strange" to the instructions God had given.

Instead of fire coming from the Lord because of His pleasure and consuming the sacrifice being offered, fire came out in judgment and consumed the ones offering the sacrifice. That day both Moses and Aaron realized in a new way the importance of discerning between the true and the false in the worship of Yahweh by carefully adhering to His Word.

Adhering to God's Word Will Keep Us from Offering "Strange Fire."

The sin of Nadab and Abihu has been repeated throughout church history and again in our day. "Strange fire" is again being offered in the House of the LORD. Yes, it is often passionate and enthusiastic and has a form of godliness, but if examined closely and compared with Scripture, it is found to be inconsistent with what God has prescribed. Those who offer this "strange fire" show contempt for Paul's admonition to the Corinthians for them to, *Learn from us the meaning of the saying, "Do not go beyond what is written"* (I Corinthians 4:6, NIV).

The primary tool for discerning between the true and the false is the Word of God. God's Word is the "canon," *i.e.*, the "standard" or "rule" by which everything else is to be measured. If we are to adequately discern between the true and the false, we must, therefore, become diligent students of the Word of God. The Charismatic Movement has fallen short in this regard, as is borne out by the following study by George Barna.

We Must Recover a Biblical Worldview.

A recent study by evangelical sociologist, George Barna, demonstrates how the American church and culture have moved away from a Biblical worldview. According to this study, only 9% of Americans hold a Biblical worldview, *i.e.*, only 9 out of every 100 Americans derive their beliefs and values from the Bible.

When Barna looked specifically at professing, born-again Christians, he found very little change in the statistics. He found that only 19% of born-again Christians in America hold a Biblical worldview. As part of this study, Barna interviewed 601 senior pastors nationwide, representing a random cross-section of Protestant churches, and found that only half of the nation's Protestant pastors hold a Biblical worldview. (*See* www.barna.org.) This lack of Biblical truth in the Church has opened the door for "strange fire" once again in the House of God.

We Must Know God and His Ways.

We can close the door on "strange fire" by familiarizing ourselves with God and His ways. How can we do this? We can do this by diligently applying ourselves to the study of His Word. The famous British evangelist, Smith Wigglesworth, once said, "I cannot know God by feelings and impressions. I can only know God by His Word." Too much of what we have called revival seems to have been based on feelings and impressions rather than the Word of God.

I have written this book because I believe the church in America is in desperate need of a Spiritual awakening that is based in Scripture. I have written this book because those who are longing for genuine *Revival Fire* must be equipped to discern between the true and the false when such revival comes.

I have written this book because I believe the church in America is in desperate need of a Spiritual awakening that is based in Scripture. I have written this book because those who are longing for genuine *Revival Fire* must be equipped to discern between the true and the false when such revival comes.

Chapter 1

MARKED BY REVIVAL FIRE

"This work of God, as it was carried on, and the number of true saints multiplied, soon made a glorious alteration in the town: so that in the spring and summer following, *anno* 1735, the town seemed to be full of the presence of God." - *Jonathan Edwards*

Praying quietly, my two friends and I walked back and forth in the tiny Sunday school room. This was something we had been doing regularly for several months without much happening, it seemed. But this afternoon was different. Suddenly, it seemed that the heavens opened, and the glory and power of God descended on us.

First, my friend, Charles, fell to floor and lay there weeping. This was followed by my other friend, Ruel, also falling under the power of God's Spirit. (We didn't know about "catchers" at the time.) I didn't fall, but as I continued walking back and forth, praising God, a sense of awe came over me and I felt a burning sensation, beginning in my *solar plexus*, spreading across my chest. Like a thick, warm liquid, it spread slowly across my chest, through my shoulders, and down my arms to my elbows. Suddenly, for the first time, I experienced a gift of the Holy Spirit and I began to prophesy.

I am not sure how long this experience lasted, but after the glory of the moment had somewhat subsided, we sat down and talked about what had just happened. Charles said that, while he was lying on the floor, the palms of his hands began to burn as if he were holding hot coals of fire. He said that the heat started in his palms and extended up his arms to his elbows. Then, suddenly, he saw clouds swirling in the room—no one else saw this—and Jesus stood before him with His hands outstretched and said,

"From this time forth, you will be used in the gifts of healings."

Ruel shared his experience and I shared mine. We were filled with joy and expectation. What was God about to do?

A Deep Hunger to Know God and His Power

I was 23 years old at this time and had recently returned home to northeast Texas after three years in the U.S. Army. Charles, too, had recently returned home after serving in the U.S. Army in Vietnam. We had both been raised in Christian homes, but had strayed from the faith as teenagers and soldiers. After returning home from military service, however, we both had rededicated our lives to Jesus and were attending the small, rural Assembly of God in Chicota, Texas, pastored by my Dad, Clarence Hyatt.

Having a deep hunger to know God and His power in a more intimate way, both Charles and I began to meet for about an hour before each church service to discuss Scripture and pray. We were also fasting, praying, and studying the Bible in our individual, personal lives. We had been seeking God in this way for several months when the visitation came that Sunday afternoon, about an hour before the regular service was scheduled to begin. That experience and what followed marked our lives forever.

Revival Breaks Out.

I don't know exactly how it happened, but what we experienced in that tiny Sunday school room flowed out and into the congregation. It wasn't that we imparted anything by preaching or laying hands on people because, at that time, we had no part in the leadership of the church. We neither preached nor prayed with people. In fact, we were both so shy that it was hard for either of us to lift our hands during praise and worship. To give even a one-minute testimony was an almost impossible challenge. So, we did not stir things up with testimonies of our experience. In fact, except that Charles told his wife, Delilah, what had happened, we told no one.

Nonetheless, a powerful work of the Holy Spirit began in that little, country church that impacted the entire area. People began to get saved, baptized in the Holy Spirit, and miraculously healed. People were even healed in their homes, as prayer was offered for them at church.

At the same time, Holy Spirit conviction was gripping people throughout the community. One night, for example, a man who was not a believer knocked on our door in the middle of the night, wanting prayer because he was under such powerful conviction by the Holy Spirit.

Word spread that God was doing something significant at the Chicota Assembly of God, and people flocked to the services from throughout northeast Texas and southeastern Oklahoma.

The Move of God
Extends Beyond the Church Building.

I recall what happened one evening when the service was about to conclude—or so we thought. It was about 10 p.m. and the little wooden building was filled with people because God was working power-fully in our midst. The pastor gave the benediction and sat down, but no one moved because a sense of awe seemed to have settled over the congregation. We sat quietly, not knowing what to do next, but sensing that God was not finished.

Then we watched as God orchestrated events. First, the front door opened and a young man walked in and made his way to the front where he knelt in prayer, giving his life to Jesus. Then, others came through the door, wanting to give their lives to Jesus. During the next hour, 17 people from outside the church were apprehended by the Holy Spirit and came through the doors and surrendered their lives to Jesus. This, of course, caused great rejoicing throughout the house.

About 11 p.m., I went outside for a breath of fresh air, where I observed with my own eyes how God was working so powerfully outside the building. Two

14

young fellows, Billy and Rayburn, known in the community as "party animals," were standing by Rayburn's car. Rayburn was bent over the hood of his car, face down, weeping. Billy was pacing back and forth, saying,

"Let's go! Let's go!"

I had never known of Billy or any of his family even to visit a church, so I assumed he wanted to get out of there. Curious, I asked,

"Where are you going?"

He looked at the church building with a mixture of longing and fear in his eyes and, in a solemn tone, replied,

"There is something in there. I've got to go in there." So I said,

"Ok. Let's go!" and walked with them to the front door. When I opened the door, they literally ran to the front of the church and fell across the altar bench, joining others, as they called out to God with all their might. I could only stand and watch in amazement. That meeting lasted until 1:30 a.m.

Teenagers Saved Without a Youth Program.

Many teenagers were saved in this revival, yet there was no youth pastor and no organized youth program. Of course, in the midst of genuine *Revival Fire*, programs are never an issue. Instead, fellowship tends to be spontaneous. One weekend, for example, a number of the young men decided that they would have an all-night outing at Pat Mayse Lake, a popular recreation area near our community. On the night of their outing, I decided to find them and see how they were doing.

It was a warm, summer night and I had my car windows rolled down as I drove slowly around the lake, passing the RVs, boats, and campers with their flickering lights. Finally, I heard loud praying in the distance, and as I followed the sound of prayer, I located them. Their hearts were so on fire for the Lord that they spent the entire night in fervent prayer. When I left them, I thought,

"The campers and boaters in the area must think that these are the strangest bunch of teenagers they have ever seen."

Such is the state of things in the midst of genuine *Revival Fire!*

I Preach My First Sermon.

My Dad recognized that God was doing a good work in Charles and me, and so he gave us responsibility to lead the regular Friday night service. It quickly became the largest meeting of the week, even exceeding the Sunday morning meeting in attendance.

People didn't come for a celebrity preacher, special music, or planned events. They came because God was working so powerfully. We had none of the things that we think are necessary for having revival today. We did not have the confidence or the skills to put on an exciting meeting. We could neither sing nor preach. We had to have God! God responded to the cries of our hearts and what happened was not the result of emotional hype and religious manipulation. It was an outpouring of God's sovereign grace and love. Gifts of the Holy Spirit flowed and lives were transformed by the power of God.

This revival lasted for about two years, and during that time, I preached my first sermon. In spite of the fact that it was only five minutes long and I had it memorized, when I finished, there was a sovereign move of the Holy Spirit. In fact, as I look back on that meeting and that revival, I realize that it was, in its entirety, a sovereign work of God's Holy Spirit.

Again, let me say that we had none of the props that we think are necessary to have revival. We had no praise band, no worship team, and no special singers. (In fact, I am convinced that good, Christian entertainment today is often mistaken for revival.) We had no famous preachers, just some down-to-earth folks pouring their hearts out to God.

Exposed to "Strange Fire" in Revival

After about two years in this revival environment and increasingly sensing a distinct call of God on my life, I left home to attend Bible school in a nearby city. In the big city, I had opportunities to attend various churches, conferences, and revival meetings.

During this time, God was requiring that I grow and change, but, at the same time, I was seeing things that concerned me in so-called "revivals." In one meeting, for example, the revivalist set up a light behind him and had people come forward and stand in his shadow, supposedly to receive healing and blessing. In another meeting, the revivalist had his own Pool

17

of Bethesda (a child's rubber swimming pool) in which he invited people to come and stand to receive healings and miracles from God. Another preacher gave out color-coded prayer cloths for different kinds of demons and sicknesses, as well as an "anointed" red string for people to wear who wanted to lose weight "miraculously." It seemed that every stunt and gimmick imaginable was being pawned off on people's naïveté in the name of revival.

About this time, 1974, I remember attending a meeting in which one of the well-known healing evangelists of the 1950s was speaking. He was calling people out of the audience, giving them prophetic words, and then literally hitting them and knocking them to the floor. He eventually came my way and asked me to step into the aisle. He gave me a prophetic word, which was quite generic, and then hit me with both hands, one on each side of my neck, as he shouted "in the name of Jesus" or something similar. I was knocked backwards, but not by the power of God! I put one foot back to keep from falling. The evangelist was obviously disgusted that I did not fall. He whirled around, and as he walked briskly up the aisle, said over the PA system,

"Preachers are the hardest people in the world to pray for!" referring to me.

There was no sense of God's peace or presence in any of this—just a preacher trying to impress people and make them think that God's power was working through him. Even as a young believer, I could see that many preachers, like this evangelist, who had once known the touch of God on their lives, were trying to continue in their flesh what God had begun in them by His Spirit. I was getting an early lesson in the need to discern between the true and the false in revival.

God Speaks to Me about His Word

It was during this time that God spoke to me about the importance of His Word in my life. I would get up at 5 a.m. each day and go to the main auditorium at 6 a.m. to spend two hours in prayer before chapel and classes. One morning, I heard the Holy Spirit speak very clearly that I was to scale back my prayer time and spend more time in His Word. In obedience, I began spending an hour each morning reading and studying God's Word, followed by an hour of prayer.

I also began reading my Bible at every opportunity. During class breaks, I would read from it. I carried it everywhere I went, and even when I would be eating alone, I would have an open Bible next to my plate and would read between bites. When eating with fellow students, I would read a passage before eating. I recall one meal with several other students in one of our apartments. Before the meal, I opened my Bible and began reading John 6 aloud. The joy of the Lord burst forth in our hearts and we laughed and praised God as I read through the entire chapter. What a meal that was, eaten together in the awareness of God's presence!

After Bible school graduation, I married Susan, a woman who loves God and His Word with all her heart and who is very sensitive to the Holy Spirit.

The first thing we did together was pioneer a new congregation and Bible school in eastern Canada. There, we saw outpourings of the Holy Spirit and lives changed by the power of God. Throughout this time, I continued to seek that delicate balance between the Spirit and the Word of God in revival.

A few years later, God led us both into higher education and we both obtained earned doctorates. Having been marked by revival, I used this educational venue as an opportunity to research revival throughout the history of the Church. Some of that research is in my book, *2000 Years of Charismatic Christianity*, first published in 1996. This volume, *Revival Fire: Discerning Between the True & the False* is more fruit of ongoing research and of my concern for the state of "revival" in the Church today.

Chapter 2

WHY THE CHURCH NEEDS A BIBLICAL REVIVAL

"I would advise no one to send his child where the Holy Scriptures are not supreme. Every institution [or revival] that does not unceasingly pursue the study of God's word becomes corrupt." - *Martin Luther*

A friend shared with me her experience visiting a revival that, because of the alleged miracles, was attracting thousands from around the world. She, being one who loves the workings of the Holy Spirit, went with an open mind, ready to embrace a genuine work of God. But she was struck by the absence of God's Word, except for a few passing references to, or quotes from, isolated passages taken out of context.

Perhaps the climax of her eye-opening experience came in the morning Bible study sessions. The theme was the believer's identity in Christ, and in one session, the teacher had everyone come to the front where she asked each person the question: Who are you? to which each was to respond: I am Jesus. With this "correct" response, the person was given a gemstone. The next morning, when my friend attended the session, she felt restrained by the Holy Spirit not to take a seat, but to stand at the back. She says,

I noticed that the teacher was telling people what to do, when to do it, and what to say — total control. As a result, people were 'flying' around the room, pretending to be eagles. There was no sense of God's presence, only control by this person. As she continued to teach, she caught my attention when she said, "I am Jesus. You are just seeing Him in a form you've never seen Him in before." Hardly able to believe what I was hearing, I checked with friends who were with me, who confirmed that I had heard correctly! At this point, our group left the room. In the lobby, I met the pastor, and after a brief exchange in which he expressed full support for what was being taught, our group departed.

This friend's story highlights the fact that the revival was not built on the serious study of Scripture, and it soon collapsed under the weight of its own sin and neglect of Biblical truth.

A Famine of Biblical Truth

My friend's experience is typical of what is occurring throughout the contemporary charismatic-revival movement where groups may spend hours "soaking," singing, prophesying and sharing their spiritual experiences, but seldom — if ever — engaging in serious, sound study of God's Word. Seeking spiritual experiences apart from Scripture is dangerous. Those taking this careless approach are, unwittingly, caught in the wake of a cultural trend that is carrying people away from the Bible to non-Christian, non-Biblical forms of spirituality

Barna has pointed out that, while Americans are forsaking a Biblical world-view, they are, at the same time, embracing new and various forms of spirituality, i.e., "strange fire." Books on angels, dreams, and spirituality abound, and popular TV shows, like *Oprah*, promise viewers spiritual fulfillment apart from Christianity and the Bible. Even Christian books on spirituality tend to be light on Biblical truth, and some have obviously borrowed concepts from New Age writers and other religions, such as Buddhism and Zen.

Medieval Mysticism — a Legitimate Model?

As part of this trend, many are looking to the medieval mystics as models of spirituality. But while many mystics are to be admired for their devotion, they are not to be followed in many of their ideas and experiences. Devoted to the hierarchical church, they shared in its lax attitude toward Scripture and brought "strange fire" into the Church. Many of their experiences have no Biblical basis and some are probably demonic. Commenting on medieval mysticism and its neglect of Scripture, Hans Kung, the most widely read Roman Catholic theologian in the world today, says,

> These new revelations not only overshadowed the Bible and the Gospel, but also Him whom the Gospel proclaims and to whom the Bible bears witness. It is striking how rarely Christ

appeared in all these "revelations," "apparitions," and "wonders." Catholics who followed in the wake of every new "revelation," which often turned out to be fantasy or deceit, and indulged their desire for sensation by looking for the latest reports of miracles—and yet who had never once in their whole lives read the Scriptures from cover to cover.[3]

Biblical Revivals Have Been the Most Enduring.

It is a fact of Church history that the most fruitful and enduring revivals began in milieus of serious Bible study, and as long as Scripture and the Christ of Scripture remained at the center, these revivals continued to produce solid converts, spiritual growth, and lasting fruit. It can also be noted that whenever Biblical truth was peripheral, with the pursuit of spiritual experience or of "revival" itself being central, the results were shallow conversions, stunted spiritual growth, and shattered lives. Two thousand years of revival history confirm the importance of making the Word of God, accurately understood and applied, the basis of all that we say and do concerning revival. As Historian Philip Schaff notes, "Every true progress in church history is conditioned by a new and deeper study of the Scriptures."[4]

---

[3] Hans Kung, *The Church* (Garden City, NY: Image Books, 1976), 257-58.

[4] Philip Schaff, vol. 7 of *History of the Christian Church*, 8 vols. (Grand Rapids: Eerdmans, 1910), 17.

Example 1: **The Methodist Revival**

The 18ᵗʰ century Methodist Revival is an example of one of the most powerful and enduring revivals of Christian history. It began with John and Charles Wesley and a number of their colleagues at Oxford University. They would meet each evening from 6 to 9 p.m. to study the Greek New Testament; and their commitment to the Word did not stop there, but extended to their personal lives as well. For example, in 1729, John Wesley wrote,

> I began to not only read but to study the Bible as the one, and the only standard of truth, and the only model of pure religion.[5]

George Whitefield's commitment to Bible study was typical of the earthly Methodists. He wrote,

> My mind now being more open and enlarged, I began to read the Holy Scriptures upon my knees, laying aside all other books and praying over, if possible, every line and word.[6]

John Walsh, a flaming evangelist and colleague of Wesley and Whitfield, memorized the entire Greek New Testament. Wesley said that one could mention any Greek word to Walsh and he could identify every place it was found in the New Testament and give its lexical meaning in the different contexts.

As a result of their diligent study of Scripture, a

---

[5] John Wesley, *A Plain Account of Christian Perfection* (London: Epworth, 1952), 6.

[6] George Whitefield, *George Whitefield's Journals* (Carlisle, PA: Banner of Truth Trust, 1960), 60.

desire burned in their hearts to live out the principles and precepts of the New Testament. They did not seek "revival," but merely sought to order their lives according to the pattern of the New Testament. As they continued to pray and to study the Bible, a revival movement broke out that transformed the British Isles and impacted the American colonies.

The grounding of the Methodist revival in Biblical truth gave it stability, resulting in much good fruit, not only in the first generation, but in succeeding generations. This is why Dr. Vinson Synan has called John Wesley "The Father," of Methodism and of all the Holiness-Pentecostal bodies that have emerged from it. The good fruit of the Biblical commitment of the early Methodists has, then, had an enduring effect.

Example 2: **The Pentecostal-Charismatic Revival**
The modern Pentecostal Revival now encircles the globe. Like Methodism, it emerged from diligent Bible study and Bible-centered living in a learning environment, a Bible school in Topeka, Kansas. In this case, the teacher and students diligently sought Biblical truth and principles, one of which was the "Bible evidence" for the baptism in the Holy Spirit. Their Biblical search resulted in an outpouring of the Holy Spirit. From there, revival fires spread around the world *via* two significant avenues: 1. Topeka to Zion City, IL; 2. Topeka *via* Houston to 312 Azusa Street in Los Angeles. The importance of Biblical truth permeated the movement from the beginning.

At Azusa Street, for example, God's Word was central and every teaching and activity had to measure up to the standard of Biblical truth. Although spiritual manifestations were expected and encouraged, all had to pass the test of Biblical truth. *The Apostolic Faith* (June-Sept., 1907), the official paper of the Azusa Street Mission, carried a statement that read,

We are measuring everything by the Word; every experience must measure up to the Bible. Some say that is going too far, but if we have lived too close to the Word, we will settle that with the Lord when we meet Him in the air.

The saints at Azusa believed that the diligent study of Scripture was the only way that fanaticism and spiritual pride could be avoided. They, therefore, urged their people to make the diligent study of God's Word a life-long pursuit.

The October 1907-January 1908 issue carried a page of questions and answers. One question asked, "Do we need to study the Bible as much after receiving the Holy Ghost?" The response was:

Yes, if not we become fanatical or many times will be led by deceptive spirits and begin to have revelations and dreams contrary to the Word, and begin to prophesy and think ourselves some great one, bigger than some other Christians. But by reading the Bible prayerfully, waiting before God, we become just humble little children, and we never feel that we have got more than the least of God's children.

Revival Is Meant to Be a Means, Not an End.

In historical movements such as these, revival was a by-product of the diligent pursuit of God and Biblical truth. In fact, revivalists such as John Wesley, George Whitfield, Jonathan Edwards, and William Seymour rarely used the word *revival*. They were after God and Biblical truth. They wanted to see His Name honored and glorified in the earth. In response to their prayers and preaching, God poured out His Spirit and awakened the masses to the realities of the Gospel. Later generations called this a "revival" or an "awakening," and it was recognized as a sovereign work of God in response to the prayers and preaching of His people.

Genuine revival does not occur by pursuing revival. True revival occurs when God's people repent of their self-serving ways and of trying to live the Christian life—and create revival—in human wisdom and strength. God then responds with a gracious outpouring of His Holy Spirit, empowering them to be His witnesses in the earth. 2 Chronicles 7:14 speaks of this principle and promises a national healing or awakening when God's people repent and turn to Him.

If My people who are called by My name will humble themselves, and pray and seek My face, and turn from their wicked ways, then I will hear from heaven, and will forgive their sin and heal their land.

This is revival based in Biblical truth. This is true *Revival Fire*.

Chapter 3

WHAT IT MEANS TO "THINK BIBLICALLY"

"We are measuring everything by the Word; every experience must measure up to the Bible. Some say that is going too far, but if we have lived too close to the Word, we will settle that with the Lord when we meet Him in the air." - *The Azusa Street Papers, June-Sept. 1907*

I have been in revival meetings where the leaders admonished the people to "turn your minds off." They went on to explain how the mind gets in the way of the work of the Holy Spirit and hinders individuals from receiving the blessing that God wants to give. They exhorted,

"If we want to see God's power at work, we must turn our minds off."

Such a mindless approach, however, is fraught with danger. Tragedies, such as the Jim Jones tragedy in Guyana, the numerous cults that have spun off from genuine Christian movements, and more recent tragedies, such as the Lakeland Revival, are essentially the result of Christians turning off their minds and refusing to think. The Biblical admonitions to "test the spirits" and to "judge" prophetic utterances require an exercise of our mental faculties. Those who turn off their minds are left vulnerable to what Scripture calls *angels of light* and *doctrines of demons.*

Jesus never told people to turn their minds off. In fact, He challenged them to think. The first word of His message was "repent," which is from the Greek word *metanoi* and literally means to "change your mind" or "thinking." Jesus also declared that the first and greatest commandment is to love God . . . *with all your mind* (Matthew 22:37). In II Timothy 4:5, Paul admonished Timothy to *keep your head in all situations* (NIV). Both Jesus and Paul would, no doubt, agree with an advertisement for Negro colleges that says: A mind is a terrible thing to waste.

We Are Transformed by
the Renewing of Our Minds

Paul revealed the important role of the mind in the believer's life when he exhorted the Christians in Rome to *be transformed by the renewing of your mind* (Romans 12:2). The word "transformed" in this passage is from the Greek word *metamorphai,* from which we get "metamorphosis."

"Metamorphosis" refers to a transformation or alteration that occurs in nature among certain species. Perhaps, the most obvious example is the change in an ugly, green caterpillar as it spins itself into a cocoon and, through metamorphosis, emerges as a beautiful butterfly. What emerges from the cocoon is not a green caterpillar wearing a butterfly suit. The very essence and nature of the creature has been changed, and the ugly, green caterpillar no longer exists. It is a new creature. Paul tells the believers in Rome that they will experience a *metamorphosis* or *transformation* through the renewing of their minds in the Word of God. Spiritual experiences are wonderful, but they will not bring the believer to God's ultimate and best. God's highest and best will be attained by the transformation that takes place through the renewing of the mind in the Word of God.

I Learn to "Think Biblically"

My first recollection of "thinking Biblically" was in the 1970s in regards to a book that was sweeping through the Charismatic Renewal Movement. Entitled *From Prison to Praise*, the book had much that was commendable in its emphasis on the importance of living a life of thanksgiving and praise. However, the author took his message to the extreme, exhorting his readers to praise God *for* everything that happened in their lives. For example, if a husband spent his paycheck on gambling and booze, leaving little or no money for food and clothing, the wife was to praise God for it. If a man's wife left him for another man, he was instructed to praise God for it. If children were using drugs and running away from home, the parents were to praise God for it. After all, Paul said that our attitude is to be one of *Giving thanks always for all things to God the Father in the name of our Lord Jesus Christ* (Ephesians 5:20).

After reading this book I began to think, "But Jesus did not praise God for everything!" When He and His disciples encountered a storm on the Sea of Galilee, He did not praise God for sending the storm into their lives. Instead, He stood in the bow of the boat, rebuked the storm, and commanded peace and stillness in the atmosphere (Matthew 8:23-27). I also recalled that He did not thank God for the religious Pharisees, but instead, He rebuked them for their spiritual blindness and hardness of heart (Matthew 23:14-16).

Then, I considered Paul. He did not thank God for everything that came his way. For example, he told the believers in Thessalonica that he would have come to them on two different occasions but Satan had hindered him (I Thessalonians 2:18).

As I mulled over all of this, comparing Scripture with the teaching of this particular author, I saw clearly that the teaching on praising God *for all things* was not compatible with the overall testimony of Scripture and that Ephesians 5:20 must be interpreted in the light of other passages. It became clear to me that there is a big difference between praising God *in all things* and praising God *for all things*. Praising God *for* all things requires the presupposition that God is the direct cause of everything that comes into our lives. I saw clearly that this was not Biblical and that Scripture teaches that there are also human and demonic factors to be considered regarding things that come into our lives. The Biblical principle is this: Concerning those things that are from God, we are told to yield and give thanks; but concerning those things that are from Satan, we are told to resist or fight against (James 4:7).

Don't Build Doctrine
on One Passage of Scripture.

The author based his idea of praising God *for* everything on Ephesians 5:20. However, to build a doctrine on one passage of Scripture is dangerous and unacceptable. In formal Biblical study, a word or idea that occurs only once in Scripture is known as a *hapax legomenon,* and it is not advisable to build a doctrine on such a single occurrence. Instead, every doctrine on which we rest our faith should be determined by the overall witness of Scripture. This is why the leaders at the Azusa Street Revival cautioned the people,

> The only safeguard from deceptive spirits is by rightly dividing the Word of God, to keep out of fanaticism. We must rightly divide the Scriptures and compare scripture with scripture so that there is no confusion, and no deceptive spirit or wrong teaching may creep in.[7]

In this same vein of thought, Martin Luther said,

"We ought to see that every article of faith of which we boast is certain, pure and based on clear passages of Scripture."[8]

---

[7] *The Azusa Street Papers: A Reprint of the Apostolic Faith Mission Publications* (Foley, AL: Together in the Harvest Publications, 1997), 60.

[8] Martin Luther, "The Babylonian Captivity of the Church," *Three*

33

Rightly Dividing the Word of Truth

Unfortunately throughout history, revival movements have been plagued by individuals, including leaders, taking isolated passages of Scripture out of context in order to defend their pet and often exotic beliefs and practices. In contemporary charismatic-revival circles, this has led to unbiblical teachings about angels, impartation, mantles, spiritual warfare, gold dust, feathers, etc.

For example, I have heard contemporary revival leaders talk about an "angel of healing," an "angel of revival," an "angel of intercession," "William Branham's angel," "John G. Lake's angel," and so on. They are, perhaps unwittingly, attributing the work of the Jesus and the Holy Spirit to angels. This sort of unhealthy preoccupation with angels was addressed by Paul in Colossians 2:18 where he chided the Colossian believers for their "worship" of angels and their naïve reliance on visions.

The word "worship" in this passage is not the normal word for "worship." It is from the Greek word *threskia*, which is found only here and in three other places where it is translated as "religion." Paul's point is that the believers in Colosse had developed a religious fascination with angels that had caused them to lose their focus on Christ. The same thing seems to have happened in the contemporary prophetic-revival movement because of a lack of Biblical study and Biblical thinking.

Treatises (Philadelphia: Fortress Press, 1957), 238.

Angels, of course, are Biblical. The Greek word is *angelos* which means "messenger," and they carry out assignments related to God's people and humanity in general. However, it is clear from Scripture that we are not to be preoccupied with seeing or encountering angels. Do you know how many angelic encounters Paul had during his life? In all of his letters, he never mentions a single one. We only know of one from Acts 27:23, where Luke tells of an angel of the Lord appearing to Paul when Paul was in a fierce storm at sea and all hope had been lost of escaping death. So, there is no need to think we must see angels on a regular basis in order to be spiritual. If that were the case, Paul was not very spiritual. We obviously need to "think Biblically" about angels.

A Renewed Mind Is a Bulwark against Deception.

When our minds are renewed in the Word of God, we will not be prone to thinking and acting in ways contrary to it. Minds renewed to think Biblically are more adept at and inclined to rightly dividing the word of truth, as Paul admonishes in II Timothy 2:15. A Christian whose mind is not renewed in God's Word may, for whatever reason, develop bizarre, enticing, and entertaining beliefs and practices based on faulty interpretations of Scripture that often results in "strange fire" once again being offered in the house of the LORD. This is one good reason for believers in the Lord Jesus to learn to "think Biblically."

Great Revivals
Have Always Engaged the Mind.

Every great revival and reformation has involved the diligent application of the mind. The Protestant Reformation (beginning in 1517), which changed the course of both Church history and world history, was a result of Martin Luther (1483-1546) and others diligently applying their minds to study and thought. Luther applied his mind and learned both Hebrew and Greek so that he was able to study and teach from the original languages of Scripture. His mind was so renewed in the Word of God that a new paradigm of salvation and church emerged that led to a reformation in Christendom.

A New Paradigm

To think Biblically means that we have so renewed our minds in the Word of God that His Word becomes the paradigm through which we interpret all of life.

To think Biblically means that our mind has become so conformed to the Word of God that it now serves as a filter through which every concept, thought, and idea passes, and all that is not commensurate with God's Word is filtered out.

To think Biblically means that our mind has become so renewed in the Word of God that it becomes the lens through which we view the world and the standard by which we judge, evaluate, and make decisions. This is what is referred to as having a *Biblical* or *Christian world-view.*

To think Biblically means that we have moved from *proof texting* to having acquired an overview of Scripture that enables us to distinguish between that which is the norm and that which is the exception; between that which is didactic teaching and that which is merely a recorded historical event.

If we are to think Biblically, our attitude must be that of the Bereans who, in Acts 17:11, were commended by the Holy Spirit because, instead of naïvely accepting what Paul and Silas preached, *they searched the Scriptures daily to find out whether those things were so.* The Berean approach of *searching the Scriptures daily* should be a vital part of every revival.

The Corinthian church was one of Paul's most gifted churches, and just as it is today, where a church is very gifted, the only safeguard from deceptive spirits is by rightly dividing the Word of God, to keep out of fanaticism. We must rightly divide the Scriptures and compare scripture with scripture so that there is no confusion, and no deceptive spirit or wrong teaching may creep in.

The Azusa Street Papers,
Jan., 1908.

Chapter 4

WHAT IS
A BIBLICAL REVIVAL?

"Every true progress in church history is conditioned
by a new and deeper study of the Scriptures."
Philip Schaff, Church Historian

The noun "revival" is derived from the old French
verb *revivre* and the Latin verb *revivere*, meaning "to
live again." It seems it was first used in a religious
sense in 1702 by Cotton Mather (1663-1728). *Revival*
is, therefore, "life again" or "life anew." The term
presupposes a loss of spiritual life and vitality. It is,
therefore, not "evangelism." *Revival* is for professing
Christians who have departed from the Gospel and
for congregations who have veered from the Gospel
and lost the life and vitality of faith in Jesus.

Historically, when nominal, formal Christians
have turned to God in repentance and faith, He has
responded by pouring out His Spirit, bringing new
life, healing, and refreshing. Therefore, in times of
revival, there is often a surprising and unusual sense
of God's presence, resulting in brokenness, repentance, and an intense enthusiasm for the things of
God. People are awakened from a spiritual dullness
and stupor to the Biblical realities of eternity, heaven,
hell, and salvation through Christ.

Revival in the New Testament

The word "revival" is not found in the New Testament. Neither Jesus, nor Paul, nor any other New Testament writer encouraged prayer for revival. "Revival" is a word that developed in the Church's history, not in the Church's origin. For example, "revival" would be out of place in the Book of Acts because there we see the Church that has just come forth in the life and power of the Holy Spirit. Only later, when the Church had institutionalized and lost the life and power of the Holy Spirit, was it appropriate to speak of the need for "revival" or "life again."

Only toward the closing days of the New Testament era, is the fading of the vibrant, spiritual life, and its consequences, becoming apparent. This is obvious, for example, in the letters to the seven churches in Revelation 2-3, written during the last decade of the first century. By then, most believers from the original generation of Christians had died and another generation had come of age. Apparently, many Christians of the new generation had slipped away from the original Gospel pattern, for Jesus says to them,

> *Nevertheless I have this against you, that you have left your first love. Remember therefore from where you have fallen; repent and do your first works . . .* (Rev. 2:4-5).

"The first love" they had left was either Jesus Himself, Who is to be the supreme object of our love and affection, or the fervent love they had known for the Lord and others when they had first become believers. Probably, it was a combination of the two.

Interestingly, the famous 19th century revivalist, Charles G. Finney, said that revival is nothing but "a return of Christians to their first love." When we, as professing Christians, realize that we have slipped away from "our first love," we have the privilege and responsibility of returning to the Lord with all our hearts. This repentance on the part of God's people always brings the gracious outpouring of the Holy Spirit. This is what we call "revival."

The Difference between "Revival" and "Evangelism"

Revival is not evangelism and evangelism is not revival. Revival is not for unbelievers, but for professing Christians who have lost the power and vitality of a living faith in Jesus and who are "Christian" in name only. Genuine revival always results in evangelism, that is, in the proclamation of the Good News and the subsequent conversion of unbelievers to Christ. This is because, in revival, Christians experience the reality of Acts 1:8 where Jesus promised to empower His followers with the Holy Spirit, enabling them to be His witnesses. This is why Finney said,

If the Church was to live only one week as if they believed the Bible, sinners would melt down before them.[9]

Whereas evangelism may result in one person or many people committing to Christ, true revival brings about community transformation through the corporate witness of a Spirit-filled Church. During the great prayer revival of 1858 major cities were impacted by the power of God. One Chicago newspaper reported,

> So far as the effects of the present religious movement are concerned, they are apparent to all. They are to be seen in every walk of life, to be felt in every place of society. The merchant, the farmer, the mechanic—all who have been within their influence—have been incited to better things; to a more orderly and honest way of life.[10]

Duncan Campbell, whom God used mightily in the Hebrides Revival of the 1950s, said,

> The difference in successful evangelism and revival is this: In evangelism, the two, the three, the ten, the twenty, and possibly the hundred make confessions of Jesus Christ, and at the end of the year you are thankful if half of them are standing. But the community remains untouched. The public houses are crowded, the dances, dancing ballrooms, are packed. But in revival, when God, the Holy

---

[9] V. Raymond Edman, *Finney Lives On* (Minneapolis: Bethany Fellowship, 1971), 104-05.

[10] *America's Great Revivals* (Minneapolis: Bethany Fellowship, n.d.), 64-65.

Ghost, comes, when the winds of heaven blow, suddenly the community becomes God-conscious! A God realization takes hold of young, middle-aged and old. So that, as in the case of the Hebrides Revival, 75% of those saved in one night were saved before they came near a meeting.[11]

Every Generation Needs Revival.

Genuine *Revival Fire* is needed in every generation because the church is continually moving away from the simplicity, purity, and power of its New Testament origins. Isaiah 53:6 says, *All we like sheep have gone astray*, and this is certainly true of the Church during the 2000 years of its existence. This "going astray" normally occurs as the Church compromises its commitment to Biblical truth and seeks to make itself acceptable to contemporary society. This compromise often happens slowly and subtly, and it always results in the dynamic truths of the Gospel being diluted or distorted so that they are more palatable to fallen, human culture. In this way, outward form, show, and ritual, in varying degrees, replace the power of a personal relationship with Jesus.

Lacking the dynamic life and power of the Holy Spirit, the Church looks for ways to connect to contemporary culture, resulting in the adoption of non-Christian beliefs and practices into the Church. This

---

[11] Duncan Campbell, *The Nature of A God Sent Revival* (Euless, TX: Successful Christian Living Ministries, n.d.) 11-12.

combining of Christian and non-Christian beliefs and practices is known as syncretism. It is what the Bible calls "strange fire" for it is something that is foreign to the Word and the Spirit of God.

So, on the one hand, when the Church is not *revived*, it adopts the ways of the world; while, on the other hand, when revival takes place, the Church impacts the world with the fire of God and the values of Heaven. The Church of our day sorely needs genuine *Revival Fire*, and a renewed loyalty to Scripture is the starting point for such revival.

Revival, therefore, is not *an end* or *goal* in itself, but rather *a means that God uses* to draw a spiritually cold and deviant Church back to the New Testament life and pattern. Consequently, it is almost impossible to find revival leaders before the 19th century who speak of the need to seek revival. Instead, they speak of their desire to know God, to see His Name honored, and to see the people of God living according to the Gospel. Out of their desire for authentic, New Testament Christianity, an outpouring of the Holy Spirit came that lifted them into faith-filled, holy living that was infused with the life of the Spirit. This is then called "revival," and because it is rooted in Scripture, it is a *Biblical* revival.

Chapter 5

AN OLD TESTAMENT
BIBLICAL REVIVAL

Your word is a lamp to my feet and a light to my path.
Psalm 119:105

The New Testament does not mention revival, but the Old Testament does. From the time of the Exodus, Israel's history consisted of repeated "backslidings" or "turnings away" from their commitment to Yahweh followed by repeated "returnings" to Him, after being overwhelmed by their enemies.

During periods of backsliding, there were prayers for God to revive His people, as well as repeated calls by the prophets for Israel's repentance. Psalm 85:5, for example, records a prayer for revival. The psalmist cries out to God: *Will you not revive us again that Your people may rejoice in you.*

Nehemiah 8:1-10:39 describes the final and, perhaps, greatest Old Testament revival. It occurred among the Jews who had returned to Israel from the Babylonian captivity to which they had been delivered because of their idolatry (*See* Jeremiah 2:26-28). This revival was ignited by a return to Biblical truth and a commitment to live out that truth to the best of their ability. The revival occurred during a celebration of the Feast of Tabernacles and was led by Ezra, the scribe, and Nehemiah, the governor. The characteristics of this revival included:

- Great hunger for the Word of God
- Repentance and confession of sin
- Brokenness with weeping
- Great joy.

CHARACTERISTIC 1:

Great Hunger for the Word of God

Ezra stood on a platform that had been erected for the occasion and read from the *Book of the Law*. Nehemiah 8:3 reports that Ezra and his associates read from morning until midday. The Hebrew phrase that is translated "from morning" literally means "from the light." This indicates that the reading took place from sunrise to noon, a period of about six hours. Ezra and his assistants not only read from the Old Testament, they also interpreted the passages for the people (Nehemiah 8:8).

As Ezra began reading from the Old Testament, the people stood *en masse*, an expression of honor and reverence for the Word of God. These readings took place daily during the seven days of the celebration. As the people listened to the commands and promises of Scripture, they were struck with conviction at how far they had departed from God and His Word. This prompted an outcry of mourning and weeping. McDowell and Reid say,

> In the light of God's commands, they realized their own failures and were challenged with their responsibilities to God. In their spiritual

remorse they made no demands for human rights or extolled their own human virtues. They were engulfed with the awesome holiness of God and their own unrighteousness. They were deeply convicted that God deserved priority in their lives and in the nation. In response, they wept over their transgressions.[12]

CHARACTERISTIC 2:
Repentance and Confession of Sin

It was the reading and explaining of God's Word that prompted the cries of repentance. It was the blazing light of truth shining brightly, exposing their sins and shortcomings. As a result, they were broken-hearted, not only for their own sins and backslidings, but also for the sins and backslidings of their mothers and fathers. At one point, they sat in sackcloth and ashes, with dust sprinkled on their heads, a sign of great sorrow and remorse (Nehemiah 9:1-2).

Their commitment to make things right is revealed in the steps they took to annul marriages and allegiances they had forged with foreigners, alliances that God had forbidden in His Word. Nehemiah 9:2 says,

> Then those of Israelite lineage separated themselves from all foreigners; and they stood and confessed their sins and the iniquities of their fathers.

---

[12] Malcolm McDow and Alvin L. Reid, *Firefall: How God Has Shaped History Through Revivals* (Nashville: Broadman & Holman, 1997), 63-64

The people confessed their sins and admitted that the evil that had befallen them (in particular, the Babylonian captivity) was because of their own sins and transgressions. Nehemiah 9:33 records a prayer of confession they made to God,

You are just in all that has befallen us; for you have dealt faithfully, but we have done wickedly.

This is true, Biblical repentance.

CHARACTERISTIC 3:

Respect and Reverence

As might be expected, lightheartedness and frivolity had no place in this revival. Both the leaders and all the people showed the utmost honor and respect for God and His Word. This was exhibited in various ways. For example, when the Scriptures were read, the people would all stand, an expression of respect. This reverential gesture later became characteristic of the Jewish people in their synagogue services.

Other expressions included lifting up their hands in worship and bowing down with their faces to the ground (Nehemiah 8:6). The bowing down with their faces to the ground was an expression of total submission to God and His will for their lives.

This was serious business with no place for silly and flippant activity. Even the joy of the Lord that emerged was not a frivolous, light moment, but a deep joy, rooted in an awesome sense of God's existence and a profound appreciation for His mercy and forgiveness.

A Release of Joy

As the people mourned and wept over their sins, Ezra, Nehemiah, and other leaders urged them to cease weeping and to rejoice in the Lord. The point was that God had seen and heard the people's remorse for their sins and He had forgiven them. It was now appropriate to celebrate the feast in the way that God had ordained in His Word. The Feast of Tabernacles was to be a time of rejoicing, expressed in eating, drinking, fellowship, and sharing with those less fortunate. In Nehemiah 8:10, the leaders said,

> Go your way, eat the fat, drink the sweet, and send portions to those for whom nothing is prepared; for this day is holy to our Lord. Do not sorrow, for the joy of the Lord is your strength.

The people received the words of Ezra and Nehemiah and went their way *and rejoiced greatly, because they understood the words that were declared to them* (Nehemiah 8:12). It is right and Biblical to experience joy when one is in a right relationship with the Almighty. This is why, throughout history, revivals have almost always been accompanied by expressions of great joy.

The Results of the Revival

This revival significantly influenced the character of the Jews as God's people. For instance, it helped solidify Jewish *monotheism*, that is, the belief in One God, so that the Jewish people would never again embrace idolatry. Further, it made a lasting imprint on many of the Jewish institutions, including: temple worship, celebration of the feasts, the synagogue, scribes, and Pharisees. In fact, according to Jewish tradition, Judaism was birthed under the leadership of Ezra, as was the guild of the scribes, which was prominent in the Gospels.[13] Also, in this revival, Scripture, rather than pagan cultures now held sway in determining standards, leading the people to make a new commitment to walk in all the promises and precepts of God's Word.

This was a Biblical revival.

---

[13] McDow and Reid, 61.

Chapter 6

JESUS & THE WORD OF GOD

And beginning at Moses and all the Prophets, He expounded to them in all the Scriptures the things concerning Himself. – *Luke 24:25*

Jesus derived His sense of identity, His lifestyle, and His mission from Scripture. He made the Word of God the basis for all that He said and did. Philippians 2:7 makes it clear that, although Jesus had existed as God from all eternity, for the sake of His incarnate sojourn and redemptive work on earth, He *emptied out* His Divine power and attributes and lived and functioned as a real human being. In this state of human frailty, He showed that the way to victory in all areas of our existence is through faith in God and His Word. The Old Testament was for Jesus, therefore, the basis of His faith, His life, and His mission.

This was clearly demonstrated when Jesus began His public ministry in Nazareth's synagogue. At that critical moment, He did not recount the story of the angels that appeared at His birth. He did not buttress His right with the prophecies of Simeon and Anna. He did not point to the audible Voice from Heaven at His baptism. Instead, He took the Scroll of Isaiah and, turning to Chapter 61, He read verse 1 and part of verse 2. He then closed the book and declared to those present, *Today, this Scripture is fulfilled in your hearing* (Luke 4:21). He, thereby, rooted His identity and mission firmly and solely in Scripture.

Scripture Was the Sole Basis of Jesus' Teaching and Preaching

Jesus' life and ministry were filled with teaching and preaching God's Word. Mark, for example, describes an incident in which so many gathered at the house where He was staying that no one else could get near the door. Mark says, *And He preached the word to them* (Mark 2:2).

On another occasion, when some told Jesus that His mother and brothers were standing outside, wanting to see Him, He replied, *My mother and my brothers are those who hear the word of God and do it* (Luke 8:210). This clearly indicates that hearing and obeying God's Word were, for Jesus, of ultimate value, even more important than being His biological mother or sibling.

When faced with doctrinal and theological challenges, Jesus would commonly respond with, *Have you not read . . .* and then point his questioners to the appropriate passage of Scripture. When, for example, the Pharisees came with a challenging question about divorce, Jesus replied, *Have you not read that He who made them at the beginning . . .,* and proceeded to point them to the Genesis account of Creation (Matthew 19:4-10). Again, when challenged concerning his disciples picking and eating corn on the Sabbath, Jesus answered with Scripture, saying, *Have you not read what David did when He was hungry . . .,* and proceeded to point out from Scripture how David had acted in a similar situation.

Jesus also appealed to Scripture in explaining the sequence of events in His life and ministry. For example, in John 13:18, He predicted His approaching betrayal by one of The Twelve and explained that it would happen, *that the Scripture may be fulfilled.* Again, at the time of His arrest in the garden, Jesus admonished Peter to put away his sword, explaining that if He wanted to escape, He could pray and the Father would give Him more than twelve legions of angels. *But*, he said, *how then could the Scriptures be fulfilled?* For Jesus, the fulfillment of Scripture was more important than His personal comfort and ease.

Jesus Defeats Satan with the Word of God.

Matthew 4:1-11 describes a 40-day period of temptation in the wilderness when Satan unleashed all that He had against Jesus. Jesus' response to each temptation again demonstrates the tremendous value He placed on the Word of God. Using it as His weapon-of-choice to defeat Satan, He responded to each temptation with a quotation from Scripture prefaced by *It is written . . . .*

Each temptation of Satan was designed to cast doubt on Jesus' identity and, therefore, began with the challenge, *If You are the Son of God . . . .* Jesus could have pulled His defense from an arsenal of amazing experiences. There was the experience of the audible Voice from Heaven at His baptism, *This is My beloved Son in whom I am well pleased* (Matthew 3:16-17). There were the words of the angel Gabriel to Mary that *He will be great and will be called the Son of the Highest* (Luke 1:31-32). There were Simeon and Anna's prophecies at the time of His birth concerning His identity and destiny. Yet, He mentioned none of these experiences.

Instead, Jesus met each temptation with Scripture, *i.e.*, with the Written Word of God. This shows that, for Jesus, the Written Word was the highest court of authority to which He could appeal. Clearly, He considered God's Word to be more reliable and of greater weight than an audible Voice from Heaven, angelic visitations, and prophetic utterances.

Jesus overcame Satan in His humanity, not in His Deity. In overcoming Satan in His humanity, He showed us humans the way to overcome the enemy of our souls and to experience victory. We, too, overcome when we, like Jesus, are able to say *it is written* to every destructive challenge and temptation we face.

The Ultimate Revelation of Jesus Is in Scripture.

Even after His resurrection, Jesus' priority was still the Word of God. In His dialogue with the two disciples on the Emmaus Road, He reprimanded them for being slow *to believe all that the prophets have spoken,* a reference to the Old Testament. Luke then says,

> *And beginning with Moses and all the prophets, He expounded to them in all the Scriptures the things concerning Himself* (Luke 24:25-27).

In other words, during this approximately two-hour walk from Jerusalem to Emmaus, Jesus spent the entire time taking these disciples from Genesis to Malachi, showing them Christ throughout the Old Testament.

Think of what He could have shared with them, but didn't! He had just come out of the tomb where He had experienced the greatest demonstration of God's power ever known. He had seen Satan's grip on humanity completely broken. He had seen mighty angels at work, rolling away the stone. But during this walk from Jerusalem to Emmaus, He apparently mentioned none of these things.

Instead, Jesus spent the entire time going through the Scriptures, making sure that they knew the Christ of Scripture. This clearly demonstrates that the greatest and most important revelation one can have of Jesus is the revelation of Him in Scripture.

Later when Jesus, at their invitation, went into the disciples' home to eat with them, He took bread, blessed it, and broke it. Suddenly, their eyes were opened and they recognized Him. At that point, He vanished from their sight. They were overcome with joy and said to one another,

Did not our hearts burn within us while He talked with us on the road, and while He opened the Scriptures to us (Luke 24:32).

Jesus Exalts His Words to the Level of Scripture.

It should not be surprising that Jesus, as God manifest in human flesh, would put His words on the same level as Scripture. In fact, He did this on numerous occasions. He declared, for example, that His words would bring Eternal Life to those who would hear and believe them.

Most assuredly I say to you, he who hears My word and believes in Him who sent Me has everlasting life, and shall not come into judgment, but has passed from death into life (John 14:24).

He also said that His word would be the standard by which humanity will be judged in the last day.

He who rejects Me, and does not receive My words, has that which judges him—the word that I have spoken will judge him in the last day (John 12:48).

This, perhaps, shines light on Matthews 7:22, where Jesus said,

Many will say to Me in that day, Lord, Lord have we not prophesied in Your Name, cast out demons in Your Name, and done many wonders in Your Name? And then I will declare to them, "I never knew you; depart from Me, you who practice lawlessness."

In other words, in the final day we will not be judged by any miracles we have performed or by how many angels and visions we may have seen, but by how carefully we have adhered to the words of our Lord. *Heaven and earth will pass away,* Jesus said, *but My words will by no means pass away.*

Will We Follow His Example?

If Jesus, our Master and Lord, so gave Himself to the study and dissemination of the Word of God, should our commitment be any less? If He, the Son of God, overcame Satan and fulfilled His mission through a 100% commitment to God's Word, can we expect to fulfill our mission and calling with anything less? In His 3½ year earthly sojourn, Jesus showed us the way to genuine *Revival Fire*. May we follow His example!

Think about it! Paul had taught, preached, and dialogued for approximately three years in this pagan city (Ephesus), and in all that time, there was no evidence that he had ever preached a sermon or spoken a word against Diana. If that were today, can you imagine the books, DVD series, documentaries, blogs, and websites that would have been produced on how to pull down the "Diana spirit" or how to overcome the "Diana spirit"?

Chapter 7

THE EARLY CHURCH &
THE WORD OF GOD

Then Paul, as his custom was, went in to them
and for three Sabbaths reasoned with them from
the Scriptures. — *Acts 17:3*

It is obvious from the Book of Acts and the Epistles
that the earliest disciples of the Risen Lord followed
His example in making Scripture the basis of everything they said and did. Even in the decision to replace Judas, Peter begins his discourse by saying, *This
Scripture had to be fulfilled which the Holy Spirit spoke
before by the mouth of David concerning Judas.* Then he
quotes from the appropriate Psalm, thus rooting their
actions in the Word of God (Acts 1:16-20).

We see this pattern again when the Holy Spirit
was poured out on the 120 in the Upper Room on the
Day of Pentecost. Peter, the spokesperson for the
fledgling group, addressed the crowd and quoted the
Old Testament prophecies of Joel in explaining what
was happening (Acts 2:16-21). He went on to direct
the crowd's attention to Jesus, and He argued from
the Old Testament, particularly the Psalms, that Jesus
was their long awaited Messiah (Acts 2:29-36).

Peter's preaching about Jesus was based on both
the Old Testament Scriptures and his eyewitness

testimony, but the evidence suggests that he held the Biblical witness of Jesus to be more reliable than His personal experience. In II Peter 1:18-21, for instance, Peter mentions his experience with Jesus on the Mount of Transfiguration when an audible voice spoke from Heaven, saying, *"This is My beloved Son in Whom I am well pleased."* Peter then says, *"And so we have the prophetic word confirmed, which you do well to take heed as a light that shines in a dark place."*

The "prophetic word" to which Peter alludes is the Old Testament. It is the basis for Peter's faith in Jesus as the Messiah, and the experience on the Mount of Transfiguration is merely a confirmation of the Scriptural testimony. Commenting on this passage, Wayne House, in the Nelson Study Bible, says,

> *We have the prophetic word confirmed* may be rephrased as "we have the prophetic word as a surer confirmation." As strong as an eyewitness account (vv. 16-18) may be, there is an even stronger confirmation that Jesus is who He said He was. The written Scriptures are even more trustworthy than the personal experience of the apostle Peter. They cast *a light that shines* like a lamp *in a dark place* and will continue to do so until the *morning star rises* (*See* Romans 13:12-14.) In other words, the truths of the Bible will continue to point to the source of truth, Christ, until He comes in glory.[14]

---

[14] H. Wayne House, NT editor, *The Nelson Study Bible* (Nashville: Thomas Nelson, 1997), 2131.

As the Gospel spread throughout Jerusalem and beyond, opportunities for witness multiplied. Regardless of the circumstances, however, the essence of the message remained the same. Whenever the disciples gave their eyewitness testimonies about Jesus, they pointed to the fact that He was the fulfillment of the promises of the Old Testament Scriptures. When Peter and John were arrested by the Jewish authorities for preaching Jesus as the Messiah, Peter boldly quoted Psalm 119:22 about the stone that the builders rejected becoming the chief cornerstone, and then applied it to the Jewish authorities and their rejection of Jesus. When Peter and John were finally released and returned to their own company, their prayer was filled with passages from the Old Testament (Acts 4:23-30). One could say that they, not only *preached* the Word, but that they also *prayed* the Word. They were consumed with the Word of God.

Paul Based His Life and Faith
Solely on the Word of God.

Even before becoming a follower of Jesus, Paul, as a Pharisee, was committed to the study and practice of the Old Testament Scriptures. His miraculous encounter with Jesus on the road to Damascus did not change his commitment to Scripture; it merely shifted and sharpened his focus to see Jesus as the goal and fulfillment of the Old Testament Scriptures.

It is clear from Acts and from his letters that Paul based his very life, identity, and mission on the promises of God in the Old Testament. For example, in the opening of his letter to the believers in Rome, he makes clear that the Gospel of Jesus Christ is something that God, *promised before through His prophets in the Holy Scriptures* (Romans 1:1-3). In his writings to the Corinthians, Paul reminds them,

> *Christ died for our sins according to the Scriptures and that He was buried and that He rose again the third day according to the Scriptures.*

In his second letter to Timothy, Paul commends him because,

> *From childhood you have known the Holy Scriptures which are able to make you wise for salvation through faith which is in Christ Jesus.*

In his letters, Paul again and again drives home his point with expressions like, *but what says the Scripture* (Romans 4:3), or *the Scripture says* (Romans 10:11), or *and the Scripture foreseeing* (Galatians 3:8). His belief in the full power and sufficiency Scripture is plainly expressed in II Timothy 3:16, where he declares,

> *All Scripture is given by inspiration of God, and is profitable for doctrine, for reproof, for correction, for instruction in righteousness that the man of God may be complete, thoroughly equipped for every good work.*

Paul's *Modus Operandi*

Paul's mode of operation in fulfilling his commission to take the Gospel to the Gentile world was to take the Old Testament Scriptures and prove from them that Jesus was the Messiah and Risen Lord. In the major cities of the Greco-Roman world to which he traveled, he would normally begin his ministry in the local Jewish synagogue where, as a Jewish teacher, he would have an opening. In describing the beginning of Paul's ministry in the synagogue in Thessalonica, Luke says,

> *Then Paul, **as his custom was**, went in to them and for three Sabbaths **reasoned with them from the Scriptures**, explaining and demonstrating that the Christ had to suffer and rise again from the dead and saying, "This Jesus whom I preach to you is the Christ"* (Acts 17:3-4).

Notice that "reasoning from the Scriptures" about the identity of Jesus as the Messiah was Paul's custom, that is, the normal way in which he carried out his ministry. The word "reasoned" is translated from the Greek word *dialogomenous*, which means "to dialogue, reason, or converse." This is very much an intellectual and rational exercise in relation to the Word of God. Paul was not just preaching a sermon or presenting a lecture, but was taking on questions and challenges concerning his message of the Messiah, as revealed in Scripture.

As was often the case wherever Paul went, in Thessalonica many believed while many others vehemently opposed him and his message. The opposition in Thessalonica, however, became so intense that the believers in Thessalonica sent Paul and Silas away by night. They traveled to Berea where they took the same approach of arguing from the Scriptures that Jesus is the Risen Messiah.

In Berea, they met a more *fair-minded* response than they had found in Thessalonica. Luke says, in Acts 17:11, that the Bereans

> *Received the word with all readiness and searched the Scriptures daily to find out whether those things were so.*

This response of the Bereans may be described as one of "being open without being naïve and being 'critical' without being judgmental." Luke, inspired by the Holy Spirit, called it being "fair-minded."

Of special note in this passage is that the final, determining factor in the Bereans' decision was not how well Paul and Silas preached or whether they performed miracles. The decisive factor in their decision was whether or not what they said was compatible with the overall testimony of Scripture. They were determined not to have any "strange fire" in their midst.

Paul Conquers Ephesus with the Word of God.

On one occasion, Paul traveled to Ephesus, one of the most idolatrous and cultic cities of the ancient world. It was the center for worship of the female goddess whom the Greeks called *Artemis* and the Romans, *Diana.* Her temple, one of the Seven Wonders of the Ancient World, was a massive, ornate structure that had taken 224 years to build. So influential was the cult that the economy of the city was actually based on the continual flow of religious pilgrims to worship at the shrine.

Paul arrived in Ephesus around the year A.D. 54, armed with the Word of God as his primary weapon. As was his habit, Paul went to the synagogue and reasoned from the Scriptures concerning the identity of Jesus as the Messiah and Risen Lord. When some of the Jews vehemently opposed him, he withdrew the disciples, *reasoning daily in the school of Tyrannus* (Acts 19:9).

The school of Tyrannus was a public lecture hall and Paul held daily meetings there in which, according to his custom, he reasoned from the Scriptures concerning the identity of Jesus as the Messiah and Risen Lord. These daily dialogues from Scripture continued for two years and, as a result, a wonderful thing happened: *All who dwelt in Asia heard the word of the Lord Jesus, both Jews and Greeks* (Acts 19:10).

As a result of Paul's daily dialogues, so many people in Ephesus were turning from Diana to Jesus that the economy of the city was collapsing. Much of the city's economic base was related to the production and sale of relics of Diana and her temple to the thousands of religious pilgrims who crowded her shrine. One leading craftsman named Demetrius, who was suffering financial loss, provoked a riot by spreading word that this newcomer, Paul, was turning many from the worship of their goddess. A crowd gathered in the outdoor stadium that would seat 25,000 people and shouted for two hours, "Great is Diana of the Ephesians."

Paul Focused on Preaching the Gospel in Ephesus.

The town clerk quieted the people and reminded them that there were courts of law through which Demetrius and others could file their grievances against Paul. He also expressed concern that if the Romans heard of this riot that they might take actions against them, since Rome did not tolerate such rowdy demonstrations. He then said something very telling about Paul's ministry in the city of Ephesus.

You have brought these men here who are neither robbers of temples or blasphemers of your goddess (Acts 19:37).

Think about it! Paul had taught, preached, and dialogued for approximately three years in this pagan city, and in all that time, there was no evidence that he had ever preached a sermon or spoken a word against Diana. If that were today, can you imagine the books, DVD series, documentaries, blogs, and websites that would have been produced on how to pull down the "Diana spirit" or how to overcome the "Diana spirit"?

Admittedly, there is a time to speak against evil; however, Christians seem to get sidetracked fighting against what is not right instead of proclaiming The Only Message that has the power to change what is not right. As someone has said, "Instead of cursing the darkness, light a candle." Paul "lit a candle" in Ephesus by proclaiming the Good News of Jesus Christ as revealed in Scripture, and it burst into a glorious, fire of the Holy Spirit that spread beyond Ephesus and throughout all of Asia Minor.

Paul's ministry in Ephesus had such impact that the economy of the city, which was based on idolatry, began to fall apart. In the same way, today in America, we will know we are seeing genuine *Revival Fire* when the drug pushers and purveyors of pornography start trying to kill the preachers and close down the churches because their businesses are drying up. Perhaps, until then, we should not be bragging too much about our "happy-hour" revivals.

We Should Follow Paul's Example.

Paul's success in Ephesus could be repeated in the 21st century, if we would learn what Paul knew: that is, that the power is in The Message of Who Christ is and what He has done for the human race. Paul knew that Jesus had defeated Satan through His death and resurrection, and that Satan, therefore, no longer exercises any legitimate authority. Paul knew the reality of Jesus' words: *All authority has been given to Me in heaven and on earth* (Matthew 28:18). He knew that Satan's ability to hold people in bondage is through lies and deception. That is why Jesus said,

> *If you continue in My word, then you are My disciples indeed; and you shall know the truth and the truth shall make you free* (John 8:31-32).

Paul did not organize spiritual warfare conferences in Ephesus and get everyone shouting at the devil, a defeated foe. Instead, He reasoned daily from the Scriptures because He knew that if people understood the truth about Jesus and what He had done, Satan's lies would be dispelled and he would no longer hold sway over their lives. This is why Paul focused his efforts in Ephesus and other pagan cities in proactively communicating the truths of God's Word. He knew that the truth of God's Word would dispel the lies by which the people were held captive. His approach was so successful that Luke says, *So the word of the Lord grew mightily and prevailed* (Acts 19:20).

Chapter 8

THE DARK AGES: NO BIBLE, NO REVIVAL

"The Scriptures are not to be given to simple and unlearned men and, above all, are not to be put into the hands of women."

- Archbiship Berthholdt of Germany

During the Middle Ages, the Scriptures were taken from the common people by a hierarchical religious leadership that claimed the exclusive authority and ability to interpret and teach Scripture. This hierarchical leadership had developed over several generations as the church institutionalized by adopting more rigid and permanent forms of structure and worship. Within that structure, the exclusive right to teach and interpret Scripture was first claimed by the bishops and eventually became centered in the bishop of Rome, that is, the pope. This claim to a supposedly God-given, authoritative, exclusive right to interpret and teach Scripture became known as the *magisterium.*

The claims of the *magisterium*, coupled with the fact that Bibles were rare and expensive, combined to keep the Bible out of the hands of the common people. In the absence of the Word of God, much "strange fire" was brought into the Church. Neither was there any significant Biblical revival because the Word of God and the Spirit of God work together. This is clear in Paul's instructions to Timothy to *take the sword of the Spirit which is the word of God* (Ephesians 6:18). In other words, the Word of God is the instrument that the Holy Spirit works through to accomplish His purpose. Where the Word of God is not held forth and proclaimed, the powerful workings of the Spirit of God will be diminished or absent.

The Effects of Institutionalization

This hierarchical structure, with its forms and offices, developed slowly as the church institutionalized after the deaths of The Twelve, Paul, and the first generation of believers. *Institutionalism* is defined as "an emphasis on organization at the expense of other factors." In the early church, institutionalism came at the expense of the freedom of the Holy Spirit and the freedom of the common people to read and interpret Scripture. With the conversion of Emperor Constantine in the 4th Century and the subsequent merger of church and state, the teaching authority of the church hierarchy became firmly established.

The exclusive right of church leaders to interpret the Scriptures was expressed by Pope Innocent III who, in 1190, declared,

> As by the old law the beast touching the holy mountain was to be stoned to death, so simple and uneducated men were not to touch

the Bible or venture to preach its doctrines.[15]

Archbishop Berthholdt of Germany echoed Innocent's ban on the Bible when he declared,

The Scriptures are not to be given to simple and unlearned men and, above all, are not to be put into the hands of women.[16]

When William Tyndale proposed an English translation of the New Testament, one priest rebuked him by saying,

"We are better without God's law than the pope's."[17]

The Absence or Lack of God's Word Resulted in Unbiblical Teachings.

The absence of mechanical printing was another factor preventing the common people from having access to the Bible. Before the invention of the printing press in the 15th Century, only hand-copied editions of the Bible were available. This meant that Bibles were both rare and expensive, making personal access to the Scriptures unlikely. In fact, for most people, the only contact with the Bible was when they heard the public reading of Scripture in church. Martin Luther saw a complete Bible for the first time in the university library when he was 20 years old, and he "rejoiced

---

[15] Schaff, vol. 6 of *History of the Christian Church*, 722-23.

[16] Schaff, vol. 6 of *History of the Christian Church*, 725.

[17] Schaff, vol. 6 of *History of the Christian Church*, 727.

that it contained so much more than was ever read or explained in the churches."[18]

The absence of God's Word among the people allowed unreliable church leaders to propagate many unbiblical doctrines and practices, *i.e.*, to bring "strange fire" into the house of God. It also gave the church hierarchy ready control of the masses, since the people had no objective standard by which to judge the teachings and actions of church leaders. Nevertheless, even during this dark period there were those who were willing to suffer in order to have the truth of God's Word.

Revival Groups Were Persecuted for the Word's Sake.

During the Middle Ages in Europe, various revival groups emerged, such as the Waldenses, the Cathari, and the Albigenses. These groups embraced the dynamic work of the Holy Spirit and called for a return to Scripture as the basis for faith and teaching.[19] These groups normally began as a result of someone obtaining access to the Scriptures.

In the case of the Waldenses, their founder, Peter Waldo (*c.* 1140 – *c.* 1218), happened to be a wealthy merchant who was able to purchase copies of the Scripture. Upon reading the New Testament, it was obvious to

---

[18] Schaff, vol. 6 of *History of the Christian Church*, 111.

[19] See Eddie L. Hyatt, *2000 Years of Charismatic Christianity* (Lake Mary, FL: Charisma House, 2002), 63-69.

him that the medieval church had sharply veered from the faith of Jesus and the early Christians.

Because these groups placed the authority of Scripture above the authority of the church, they came under terrible persecution from church authorities. Branded as heretics, they were imprisoned, tortured, and burned at the stake, and their writings were destroyed. This means that most of what we know about these groups is based on the writings of their enemies who painted them in the worst possible light. Nonetheless, the notes that have been preserved from numerous heresy trials show that the people who comprised these groups were well-versed in Scripture. Records show that they constantly and consistently appealed to Scripture to refute the charges of their accusers. In reaction to this, at the Synod of Toulouse in 1229, the Roman Catholic Church issued a formal ban, forbidding lay people the use of vernacular translations of the Bible.

Courageous Individuals
Take a Stand for the Word of God.

Even with the official ban in force, other groups and individuals continued to risk their fortunes and lives to put the Bible into the hands of the people.

- **John Wycliffe** (1328-1384), an Englishman known as the "Morning Star of the Reformation," declared that the Bible, instead of the pope, was the sole authority for the believer. By 1384, with help from supporters, he was able to produce translations of the Old and New Testaments from the Latin Vulgate into English.

- **John Huss** (1373-1415), the pastor-priest of Bethlehem Chapel in Prague, preached justification by faith and the supreme authority of Scripture 100 years before Luther.

- **William Tyndale** (1494-1536), another Englishman, produced the first English translation of the New Testament directly from the Greek in 1525.

Wycliffe, Huss, Tyndale, and others paid dearly for their commitment to Scripture. Wycliffe's teachings were officially condemned and he was forced to retire from writing and preaching. Thirty-one years after his death, in 1415, the Council of Constance declared Wycliffe a heretic and ordered that his bones be dug up and burned. The same council declared John Huss a heretic and he was burned at the stake the same day. William Tyndale was also condemned as a heretic in 1536. He was tied to the stake, strangled, and his body burned. His dying words were,

"Lord, open the king of England's eyes."

Medieval Mysticism

Medieval mysticism stood somewhere between the evangelical revival groups of the Middle Ages and the church hierarchy. Like the Waldenses, Albigenses, and Cathari, Christian mystics arose in reaction to the lifeless, outward forms of the medieval church. Unlike the evangelical revival groups, however, the mystics gave their ultimate allegiance to the pope and the institutional church, rather than to Scripture. Those who did use Scripture employed the allegorical method of interpretation by which Scripture can be made to say whatever the interpreter wants it to say. These attitudes resulted in many unbiblical practices and experiences being embraced by the mystics, such as, but not limited to:

- A mystical union of the soul with God
- An ascetic withdrawal from the world
- Unhealthy preoccupation with suffering
- The rejection of rational thinking.

CHARACTERISTIC 1:
A Mystical Union of the Soul with God

The goal of the medieval mystic was a union of the human soul with God in which the individual would "swim in the wild waves of the ocean of God's being."[20] This mystical union could only be achieved in a state of quietness and contemplation, "the quiet dark in which all who love God lose themselves," as one mystic put it. As aids in achieving this contemplative state, various postures and techniques for prayer and meditation were employed. Some were quite remarkable. Gregory Palamas, a 13th Century monk, stressed quietness and stillness in the pursuit of this union with God. As an aid to concentration, he recommended that the chin rest on the chest, with

---

[20] Schaff, vol. 6 of *History of the Christian Church*, 276.

the eyes fixed on the navel.[21]

An Ascetic Withdrawal From the World

In its merger with Monasticism, mysticism took on an ascetic character in which withdrawal from the world and the normal routines of daily life was empha- sized. The monastery and the convent thus became the ideal places where mysticism could be studied and applied. In the monastery, Luther diligently sought to find peace with God through ascetic and mystical practices but was frustrated in these at- tempts. After finding peace with God through the revelation of the gospel in the Scriptures, he wrote, "If ever a monk got to heaven by monkery, I would have gotten there."

An Unhealthy Preoccupation with Suffering

An unhealthy preoccupation with suffering characte- rized medieval mysticism. Some mystics, such as Julian of Norwich (1342-ca.1416), considered one of the greatest English mystics, prayed to be deathly sick, thinking that through such suffering she could better identify with Christ in His sufferings.

Not having an opportunity to suffer for Christ, as did the early Christian martyrs, many mystics pur- sued a self-inflicted martyrdom. For example, Henry

---

[21] Tony Lane, *Harper's Concise Book of Christian Faith* (San Francis- co: Harper & Row, 1984), 64.

Suso (d. 1366), a German Dominican mystic who gained fame for his sanctity and devotion, wore an undergarment studded with 150 sharp tacks that, he said, felt as if he were lying in a nest of wasps. He also made a wooden cross to which he affixed 30 spikes and on this he lay every night for eight years. To intensify his suffering, he affixed seven sharp needles to the cross, and for a long time, he daily inflicted himself with two penitential drills. In these exercises, he would tie the cross to his back and beat upon it with his fist until the spikes and needles penetrated the flesh and the blood flowed down to his feet.[22]

This unhealthy preoccupation with suffering, and the belief that it produced a cleansing effect on the soul, gave rise to writings such as *The Dark Night of the Soul* by John of the Cross (1542–91), a Spanish mystic and close friend of Theresa of Ávila (1515-1584).

CHARACTERISTIC 4:
The Rejection of Rational Thinking

Medieval mysticism also rejected reason and rational thinking, accessing these as hindrances to the soul achieving unity with God. For example, around the year 500, an anonymous individual authored a very influential book entitled *Mystic Theology* in which he said,

> I counsel thee in the earnest exercise of mystic contemplation, that you leave the senses and activities of the intellect and all that the senses

---

[22] Schaff, vol. 6 of *History of the Christian Church*, 263-64.

or intellect can perceive. Having laid your understanding to rest, strain as far as you can toward a union with Him whom neither being nor understanding can contain. So shall you be led upwards to the Ray of that divine Darkness which surpasses all existence.[23]

The writings of this individual, who falsely claimed to be the Dionysius who was one of Paul's converts in Athens (Acts 17:34), have obvious parallels with pagan forms of mysticism, particularly in Neoplatonism.[24] Dr. Justo Gonzalez describes this work as, "An explanation of basically Neoplatonic mysticism in which the religious life consists in an ascending vision of God.[25]

Mysticism Does Not Align with the Teachings of Jesus or the New Testament.

Of course, neither Jesus nor Paul advocated the rejection of the intellect or rational thinking. In fact, Jesus said that we are *to love God with all our . . . minds* (Matthew 22:37). Paul's mode of operation in fulfilling his call to the Gentiles involved the use of logical thinking as he *reasoned daily* in the synagogues and in the school of Tyrannus concerning the identity of Jesus (Acts 17:2-3; 19:9-10).

---

[23] Tony Lane, *Harper's Concise Book of Christian Faith* (San Francisco: Harper & Row, 1984), 56.

[24] From Eddie L. Hyatt, "Some Thoughts on Mysticism," at BiblicalAwakening.blogspot.com.

[25] Gonzales, 40.

It is the carnal mind that is against God, not the mind *per se*. The answer is not to reject the mind and rational thinking, but to renew the mind in God's Word as Paul admonishes in Romans 12:2. God's Word and Spirit will often transcend human reason, but they will never violate it or seek to eliminate it.

Medieval mysticism is out of touch with Jesus and the New Testament in terms of prayer, as well. Jesus, for example, does not advocate any form of mystical prayer. He does not teach any postures or techniques for prayer and meditation. Neither is there any mention of silence or contemplation. Instead, He emphasizes a relational approach to God in which prayer is simple conversation with a loving, benevolent Being whom He calls *Abba*, an endearing term used only by children for the father in the Jewish household.

For Jesus, oneness with God is not a mystical union of one's being with God, but a practical oneness of will and purpose, culminated by the indwelling Holy Spirit and Word of God in one's life.

Another point of divergence with Jesus and New Testament Christianity is that Jesus does not call His disciples to withdraw from the world into solitude and contemplation. Instead, He promises a baptism in the Holy Spirit that will empower His followers to prophetically engage the world as His witnesses.

Neither does Jesus teach progressive stages of cleansing through darkness and suffering, as did the mystics. Instead, He emphasizes the Word of God as an agent of cleansing. For example, He says to His disciples, *You are already clean through the word I have spoken to you* (John 15:3). And He prays to the Father, *Sanctify them by Your truth, Your word is truth* (John 17:17).

Medieval mysticism, in fact, seems to have more in common with the mysticism of the East than it does with Biblical Christianity. This is why Kung says,

> And yet we must realize that mysticism is not a specifically Christian phenomenon. Not only is mysticism older than Christianity; it also comes from far away. Mystical religion had already come into being at a very early stage – in the late Vedan period – in India.[26]

The Reformers Were Opposed to Mysticism.

Martin Luther and other Reformers, especially the Anabaptists, were open to supernatural, mystical experiences, but they subjugated their experiences to Scripture. For example, one day while Luther was praying intensely, a bright vision suddenly appeared on the wall. The vision seemed to be of Jesus, revealing the wounds of His passion and looking directly at him. At first, Luther thought it must be a heavenly revelation, but he changed his mind because the image in the vision was not compatible with the Christ he knew from Scripture. He said,

> Therefore I spoke to the vision thus: "Avoid you, confounded devil. I know no other Christ

---

[26] Hans Kung, *Christianity: Essence, History, and Future* (New York: Continuum, 1995), 448.

than He who was crucified, and who in His Word is presented unto me." Whereupon the image vanished, clearly demonstrating from whom it came.[27]

Although the mystics' devotion may be admirable, their approaches to spirituality must be read with discerning caution and carefully compared with Scripture. The Reformers and Revivalists of the 16th Century did not consider the medieval mystics to be their predecessors, but, rather, modeled their faith and spirituality after Jesus and the New Testament. We would be wise to follow their example.

An Amazing Prophecy

In 1415, when John Huss was being led to the stake to be burned for preaching that Scripture is the final authority for the believer, he spoke an amazing prophecy. In Bohemian, his surname, "Huss," sounds like "goose," and in his native tongue, he spoke to his tormentors a prophecy which was heard by many of the spectators. He said,

"You may burn this goose, but one hundred years from now, a swan will arise that will frighten all you vultures."

Martin Luther came along one hundred years later, and when he read this prophecy, he was encouraged and believed that Huss, by the Spirit, had spoken of him and his work of Biblical reformation.

---

[27] Martin Luther, *Table Talk* (Gainesville, FL: Bridge-Logos, 2004), 138-39.

I know full well that I have been very outspoken. I have made many suggestions that will be considered impractical. I have attacked many things too severely. But how else ought I to do it? I am duty bound to speak. I would rather have the wrath of the world upon me than the wrath of God. The world can do no more than take my life.

Martin Luther

Chapter 9

THE IMPACT
OF MARTIN LUTHER
AND THE REFORMATION

"I simply taught, preached, wrote God's Word;
otherwise I did nothing. The Word so weakened
the papacy that never a prince or emperor did
such damage to it. I did nothing. The Word did it
all." - *Martin Luther*

God used Martin Luther (1483-1546) to turn the church's
attention to Scripture as the basis of faith, doctrine,
and life. His rallying cry against a church hierarchy
that claimed authority in all areas of faith and doctrine
was *sola Scriptura*, meaning "only Scripture" or
"Scripture alone." When confronted by church authorities concerning his right to challenge the existing
order, Luther announced that his source of authority
was not pope, bishops, or church councils, but the
Word of God. In the ensuing battle, he said his one
weapon would be Scripture—*Scripture alone.*

This emphasis by Luther and the Reformers on
the sole authority of the Word of God opened the
way for all the great revivals of the modern era.
Luther's work broke the paralyzing grip of a religious hierarchy that had quenched the Spirit and
kept the Scriptures from the people. His emphasis on

the priesthood of all believers unleashed the common people to pray and expect answers from God. Had there had been no Luther, there would have been no Methodist Revival, no Great Awakenings, no Cane Ridge, and no Pentecostal-Charismatic revival.

Luther's Early Life

Luther was born into a poor, German peasant family in 1483. He was taught to pray to God and the saints, and to revere the church and the priests. He was also told frightful stories about the devil and witches.

One day, in 1505, when he was 22, Luther was caught in a terrible thunderstorm and feared for his life. In a state of panic, he made a vow to become a monk if his life was spared, which it was, and true to his vow, he entered the Augustinian monastery at Erfurt that same year.

As a monk, Luther's chief concern was to become a saint and earn a place in Heaven. He diligently observed the minutest details of discipline, living a very austere life and learning the principles of mystical prayer and meditation. His days were spent in reading and studying, prayer and fasting, night watches, and self-mortifications. His fellow monks esteemed him as a model of sanctity and envied his self-denial. He later said, "If ever a monk got to heaven by monkery, I would have gotten there." In spite of his austere lifestyle and many religious works, he found no peace with God.

While still a monk, Luther continued his studies, and in 1507, he was ordained to the priesthood and celebrated his first mass. Then, in 1511, he was sent to Wittenberg to be the professor of Bible at the newly formed university. In the same year, he received his doctor of theology degree.

In this teaching position, he began to lecture in the vernacular on the books of the Bible. To do so intelligently, he began to study the Bible in the original languages. It was while teaching through the New Testament, particularly Romans and Galatians, that Luther began to see the truth of justification through faith in Jesus alone.

Luther Learned the Power of God's Word.

It was the power of God's Word, and the revelation therein of being made righteous before God through faith in Jesus that brought Luther into a place of peace with God. A reading of Romans 1:17 convinced him that only through faith in Christ could a person become just before God and experience peace. This was revolutionary, for the church taught that one was saved through submission to the church and by receiving the sacraments from an ordained priesthood.

Luther, being also the parish priest in Wittenberg, preached these revolutionary doctrines from the pulpit, as well as in the classroom. As a result, before long, his sermons were being printed and distributed throughout Germany, arousing great interest among the masses and great consternation among church officials. Ordered by his superiors to stop preaching and publishing these "heretical" doctrines, Luther had to decide if he would obey God or man. By now, it was clear to him that his source of authority was the Word of God and that he must preach it even if the devil and the entire world opposed him.

When he continued to preach and teach the truths he had learned from Scripture, Rome excommunicated him and ordered that all of his books and tracts be confiscated and burned. He was condemned as a heretic at the Diet of Worms (1521), and anyone knowing his whereabouts was instructed to inform the nearest authorities so that he could be arrested. By now, however, Luther's writings had gained such favor with the masses that neither pope nor emperor dared to apprehend him. Later in life, explaining how he was able to succeed in the face of such formidable opposition, Luther credited his success to the power of God's Word. He said,

> I only urged, preached, and declared God's Word, nothing else. And yet while I was asleep, the Word inflicted greater injury on popery than prince or emperor ever did. I did nothing; the Word did everything.[28]

Confronting An Errant Spirituality with Scripture

In addition to confronting both wrong doctrine and the church hierarchy with Scripture, Luther also challenged aberrant spirituality—beliefs and practices that had become divorced from Scripture, i.e., "strange fire."

---

[28] Schaff, vol. 7 of *History of the Christian Church*, 389.

For example, while Luther was in hiding in the Castle of Wartburg after his excommunication and condemnation at the Diet of Worms, two men from Zwickau, known as the Zwickau Prophets, visited Wittenberg claiming to have had divine visions, dreams, and visits from the angel Gabriel. They wowed the people with their revelations and began taking the reform movement in Wittenberg in a radical direction that was not compatible with Scripture.

Melancthon and Luther's other colleagues were unable to stop them, and when Luther heard what was happening, he put his life at risk and returned to Wittenberg. He preached eight sermons on eight consecutive days, challenging with Scripture the visions and dreams of the prophets from Zwickau.

> In plain, clear, strong, scriptural language, he refuted the errors without naming the errorists."[29]

It soon became obvious to the people that the two men were in error. The prophets, realizing they had lost their influence, left Wittenberg and never returned. One of Luther's colleagues wrote to the Elector of that region,

> Oh, what joy has Dr. Martin's return spread among us. His words, through divine mercy, are bringing back every day misguided people into the way of truth. It is as clear as the sun, that the Spirit of God is in him, and that he returned to Wittenberg by His special

---

[29] Schaff, vol. 6 of *History of the Christian Church*, 388.

providence.[30]

Opposing Miracle Claims for Monetary Gain

Luther also challenged the Roman Church hierarchy for using miracle claims within monasticism and mysticism for monetary gain. Luther, of course, believed in miracles, but he believed that miracles must be in line with Scripture. In his estimation, many of the miracle claims within monasticism and mysticism simply did not pass the test of Biblical truth, *i.e.*, they were "strange fire."

In his book, *To the Christian Nobility of the German Nation,* Luther rebuked church leaders for promoting extra-Biblical miracles. These included claims that certain hosts (*i.e.*, communion wafers) bled and that a statue of the Virgin Mary had been miraculously created. Great crowds flocked to the places where these alleged miracles were supposed to have occurred and much money was collected in offerings, in fees for masses, and from the sale of amulets and indulgences. Luther was incensed and thundered his rebuke:

> Oh, what a terrible and heavy reckoning those bishops will have to give who permit this devilish deceit and profit by it. They should be the first to prevent it and yet they regard it all as a godly and holy thing. If they had read the Scripture as well as the damnable canon law, they would know how to deal with this matter! The miracles that happen in these places prove

---

[30] Schaff, vol. 6 of *History of the Christian Church,* 390.

nothing, for the evil spirit can also work miracles, as Christ has told us in Matt. 24:24.[31]

Luther's Personal Faith in the Miraculous

Luther believed in miracles and saw miraculous answers to his prayers. This motivated him to write a divine healing service for Lutheran congregations. His faith also made a difference when his friend and colleague, Philip Melanchthon, was dying. Luther prayed over him, quoting all the Scriptures he could call to mind related to faith and healing. Then he took Melanchthon by the hand and said,

"Be of good courage, Philip! You shall not die." Melancthon immediately revived and soon regained his health. Later, he said,

"I should have been a dead man had I not been recalled from death itself by the coming of Luther."[32]

The noted historian, Philip Schaff, said of Luther,

"He lived and moved in the heart of the Scriptures; and this was the secret of his strength."[33]

Luther himself once said,

What greater wickedness, what greater contempt of God is there than not believing His promise? For what is this but to make God a liar or to doubt that He is truthful?—that is, to

---

[31] M. Luther, "To the Christian Nobility of the German Nation," *Three Treatises* (Philadelphia: Fortress Press, 1957), 75-76.

[32] A. J. Gordon, *The Ministry of Healing*, (Harrisburg: Christian Publ., 1961), 94.

[33] Schaff, vol. 7 of *History of the Christian Church*, 295.

ascribe truthfulness to one's self but lying and
vanity to God.[34]

Reformation Opened the Way for Revival.

It was no coincidence that the Reformation, with its
emphasis on Scripture, came in the wake of the invention of the printing press, with the Bible being the
first book to be printed. For the first time in history,
God's Word could be mass-produced and made
available to the common people.

With the Word of God now available on a scale
hitherto unknown, Luther and other reformers emphasized education for the masses, primarily so that
they could read the Bible. They understood that getting
God's Word into the hands and hearts of the people
was the key to on-going reformation throughout the
Church.

The invention of the printing press and Luther's
success in directing the church's attention back to
Scripture did more to change the course of history
than any events since the birth of Christ and the conversion of the apostle Paul. Even secular historians
understand this, and *Time Warner*, in the year 2000,
named Gutenberg's invention of the printing press
and Luther's instigation of the Reformation as the
numbers one and three most important events of the
past millennia.

---

[34] Martin Luther, "The Freedom of a Christian," *Three Treatises*
(Philadelphia: Fortress Press, 1957), 285.

Luther & Anti-Semitism

Luther made unfortunate and inexcusable statements about the Jews of his day, which must be recognized and rejected by modern believers. However, the attempt by some contemporary writers to paint Luther as a primary cause of modern anti-Semitism and a reason for Jewish hatred in Nazi Germany goes beyond the historical record and may well be fueled by a sinister attempt to discredit Luther and, thereby, rob the Church of the vital and critical contributions he made.

Luther's Love & Support for the Jewish People

Luther once stated that he admired—indeed, loved—the Jewish people. In his book of 1523 entitled *That Jesus Christ Was Born a Jew*, he attempted to win Jews to the gospel message of Christ, and in that context he also advocated humane treatment for them in the face of widespread anti-Semitism throughout Europe. He reminded Christians that Jesus Christ was born a Jew and that "we in turn ought to treat the Jews in a brotherly fashion."

Luther continued to support the baptized Jew, Bernard, when he fell on hard times in 1531 and had to leave his family because of his debt. Luther and Melanchthon each cared for one of his children and continued this support for many years. Even though it posed a financial hardship for him, Luther said he did it because "he felt obligated to do good to Bernard as a member of the Jewish church." Bernard also served as a messenger for Luther on numerous occasions.

Luther reported on one occasion that three rabbis visited him because they had heard of his interest in the Hebrew language and hoped to reach an agreement with him. However, they rejected Luther's argument that the messianic prophecies of the Old Testament point to Jesus Christ. Nonetheless, because Jews were forbidden to travel in that part of Germany, Luther gave them a letter of introduction in which he asked "for Christ's sake" that they be granted free passage. Because of his mention of Christ, they refrained from using the letter.

To another Jewish friend, Luther argued that the gospel had to be of God; for how else could it be explained that Gentiles, who hate Jews, worship a Jewish king, much less a crucified one.

Luther Encounters Anti-Christian Polemics

Luther was eventually attacked by Jewish writers who vilified him for his attempts to win them to Christ. His writings such as, *That Jesus Christ Was Born a Jew*, were maligned and held up to ridicule. Luther's response was, at first, mild. He replied, "For the sake of the crucified Jew, whom no one will take from me, I gladly wanted to do my best for you Jews, except that you abused my favor and hardened your hearts."

Luther's attitude toward the Jews obviously hardened as he entered more extensive dialogues/debates with Jewish rabbis on the Scriptures and the Messiah. Luther had hoped that, through these debates, the Jews would be won to faith in Christ. Through these debates, however, Luther was exposed to rabbinical writings that maligned Jesus and Christianity. He was horrified to read of Jesus being vilified as the illegitimate son of a whore and a cabalistic magician who was exposed for his trickery and put to death. Having been taught from childhood to reverence and honor God and Jesus and Mary, he responded with both anger and fear. He wrote,

> I am still praying daily and I duck under the shelter of the Son of God. I hold Him and honor Him as my Lord, to whom I must run and flee when the devil, sin or other misfortune threatens me, for He is my shelter, as wide as heaven and earth, and my mother hen under whom I crawl from God's wrath. Therefore, I cannot have any fellowship or patience with obstinate blasphemers and those who defame this dear Savior.

When he found the rabbis to be obstinate in their positions, he finally gave up any hope of the Jews coming to Christ *en masse*. And with them entertaining such blasphemous views of Christ, he gave up any hope of Christians and Jews being able to live together in harmony.

Although Luther should have responded in the spirit of the One he proclaimed (Who had prayed for His tormenters at the cross, "Father forgive them, they know not what they do") he, instead, reacted with anger and fury and wrote a treatise entitled *On the Jews and Their Lies*. The word *Lies* in the title referred to the Jewish diatribes against Jesus, Mary, and the Triune God. The third section of this book contains the diatribes that he fulminated against the Jewish people.

The Significance of the Religious & Social Setting

Without excusing Luther, we must, nonetheless, understand that the medieval period was not a time of civility and tolerance. The medieval Roman Church, of which Luther was a part, imprisoned, tortured, and put to death those that deviated from the official teachings of that church. Luther himself was declared a heretic and excommunicated because of his teachings on justification by faith and the priesthood of all believers. But for God's help, he too would have been imprisoned and put to death. Neither possessing nor desiring material weapons with which to fight his enemies, Luther said he sought to overwhelm them with words. He thus used logic, ridicule, compassion, laments, threats, satire, hyperbole, and every form of speech in making his arguments. He did not hold back but unleashed a torrent of words against the "Romanists," the "Turks," the "Anabaptists," the "Jews" and all that he considered to be enemies of the gospel of Christ. Those on the other side used the same sort of abusive language against him.

Yes, *On the Jews and Their Lies* contains abusive and violent language; but Luther used the same sort of language against the Catholics, the Anabaptists and even his own German people whom he called "brutal, furious savages" who were spiritually "deaf, blind, and obdurate of heart." His recommendation that the Jews be expelled from Germany was his same stance toward Catholics, Turks (Muslims), and Anabaptists. In this he was consistent with the idea, he retained from Roman Catholicism, of a territorial state church that holds the right and responsibility to forcefully maintain the purity of the faith in a particular region. It was smaller sects, such as the Anabaptists and Quakers, who championed the cause of voluntary congregations, free to function in an open environment without coercion by a state church. Such an idea of openness and tolerance was, however, new and novel to the medieval period and it was one in which Luther fell short in his battles with the Jews and Anabaptists.

Respecting Luther Despite His Shortcomings

The eminent Lutheran scholar, Martin Brect, points out that Luther's invectives against the Jews were not based on race but on a disagreement in theology. He says that Luther, therefore, "was not involved with later racial anti-Semitism."[35] Nonetheless, Luther's misguided invectives had the unfortunate result of him becoming identified with the church fathers of anti-Semitism and they provided fodder for modern anti-Semites who cloaked their hatred of the Jews in the authority of Luther.

While we acknowledge Luther's failures, we must not fall into the trap of rejecting him and everything he stood for. That would be tragic. On their website (www.lcms.org), The Lutheran Church, Missouri Synod has graciously and wisely denounced Luther's anti-Jewish invectives while recognizing the vital and critical contributions he has made to all of Christendom. They also point out Luther's conciliatory tone in his last sermon when he said of the Jews, "We want to treat them with Christian love and to pray for them, so that they might become converted and would receive the Lord."

In 1545, about one year before his death, Luther revised a hymn that had blamed the Jews for the

---

[35] Martin Brect, James L. Schaaf, trans., *Martin Luther: The Preservation of the Church* 1532-1546 (Minneapolis: Fortress Press, 1993), 351.

death of Christ (a common claim by the medieval church), removing the invective against the Jews. Luther's revised version reads,

> T'was our great sins and misdeeds gross
> Nailed Jesus, God's true Son, to the cross.
> Thus you, poor Judas, we dare not blame,
> Nor the band of Jews; ours is the shame.

If Luther were living today in this more tolerant and civil era, and with the Jews back in their homeland, he might well be one of their biggest supporters.

Chapter 10

HISTORICAL EXAMPLES
OF BIBLICAL REVIVAL

"While God was so remarkably amongst us by His Spirit, there was no book so delightful as the Bible; especially the book of Psalms, the Prophecy of Isaiah, and the New Testament. Some, by reason of their love to God's word, at times have been wonderfully delighted and affected at the sight of a Bible." - *Jonathan Edwards*

With the masses now reading the Scriptures, particularly the New Testament, hearts were stirred to know and experience the Christianity of the Bible. This led to private and corporate times of prayer and more Bible study, as many sought a return to what was often called "primitive Christianity." This search for the God of the Bible and the Christianity of the New Testament opened the way for the revivals that have been such a vital part of the Church since Luther and the Reformation. R. A. Torrey is correct to say, "The history of the Church of Jesus Christ on earth has been very largely a history of revivals," and this is especially true of the modern era. With this in mind, insights into the character of Biblical revival can be gained from three historic revivals: The Methodist

Revival, the First Great Awakening, and the 19th Century revivals led by Charles Finney.

John Wesley and the Methodist Revival

The Methodist Revival transformed the entire British Isles and probably saved England from a bloody revolution such as occurred in neighboring France during that century. The revival must be traced to John Wesley (1703-1791), his brother Charles (1707-1788), George Whitefield (1713-1770), and others meeting together at Oxford University for prayer, mutual exhortation, and the diligent study of the Greek New Testament. Their openness to the Holy Spirit and their commitment to the study and exposition of Biblical truth gave early Methodism a power and stability rarely known in revival movements.

As the early Methodist preachers proclaimed the good news, often outdoors in the open air, thousands responded. Although they did not give altar calls or have prayer lines, manifestations such as falling, shaking, convulsing, weeping, shouting, and roaring would take place throughout the crowd as they preached. A typical entry in Wesley's journal reported a meeting in which,

> My voice could scarce be heard amidst the groanings of some, and the cries of others, calling aloud to Him that is 'mighty to save.'"[36]

---

[36] John Wesley, vol. 1 of *The Works of John Wesley*, 14 vols. (Grand Rapids: Baker, n.d.), 207, May 1, 1739.

Also, Whitfield, in his journal, records many manifestations occurring in his meetings. For example, in Delaware, the people's response to his message was almost overwhelming. He wrote,

> Never did I see a more glorious sight. Oh what tears were shed and poured forth after the Lord Jesus. Some fainted; and when they had got a little strength, they would hear and faint again. Others cried out in a manner as if they were in the sharpest agonies of death. After I had finished my last discourse, I was so pierced, as it were, and overpowered with a sense of God's love, that some thought, I believe, I was about to give up the ghost. How sweetly did I lie at the feet of Jesus.[37]

Both Wesley and Whitefield believed in a lively, "warmed heart" Christianity. However, both expressed concern that the people not become preoccupied with manifestations lest they be drawn away from Scripture into "strange fire". Along these lines, in a letter dated June 25, 1739, Whitfield exhorted Wesley neither to require nor encourage manifestations because it would "take people away from the written word." He wrote,

> I think it is tempting God to require such signs. That there is something of God in it, I doubt not. But the devil, I believe, does interpose. I think it will encourage the French

---

[37] George Whitefield, *George Whitefield's Journals*, (Carlisle, PA: Banner of Truth Trust, n.d.), 425.

Prophets, take people away from the written word, and make them depend on visions, convulsions, etc., more than on the promises and precepts of the gospel.[38]

Wesley tells of talking to several of his followers about their spiritual experiences. These discussions point to the fact that Biblical truth was the standard by which he judged these experiences. On this basis, some experiences received his stamp of approval, while others did not. Several people reported experiencing an overwhelming sense of God's peace, while others told of love and joy. Wesley said,

"And thus far I approved of their experience because agreeable to the written word."[39]

Others described experiences for which Wesley could find no basis in Scripture. Some, for example, said they felt the blood of Christ running up their arms, or going down their throat, or pounding like warm water upon their chest and heart. Wesley said,

I plainly told them the utmost I could allow, without renouncing both Scripture and reason, was that some of these circumstances might be from God (though I could not affirm they were) working in an unusual manner, no way essential to either justification or sanctification; but

---

[38] Whitfield, 497.

[39] Wesley, vol. 1 of *Works of John Wesley*, 426-27, Sept. 6, 1742.

that all the rest I must believe to be the mere empty dreams of an heated imagination.[40]

Throughout history, revivals have repeatedly fallen prey to what the ancients called "enthusiasm," which can be understood as the forsaking of reason and Biblical truth in pursuit of sensational, spiritual experience. It is the same as that which Scripture calls "strange fire."

Although Wesley was open to—and even defended—spiritual manifestations, he warned the people against "enthusiasm" and he continually directed the people's attention back to Scripture. His standard rule was:

> Try all things by the written word, and let all bow down before it. You're in danger of enthusiasm every hour, if you depart ever so little from the Scripture: yea; from that plain, literal meaning of any text, taken with the context.[41]

Jonathan Edwards and the Great Awakening

The Great Awakening (1726-1750) transformed colonial America from a land fraught with spiritual and moral apathy to a land ablaze with the light and love of Jesus Christ. The name most often associated with this transforming era is Jonathan Edwards (1703-1758). A child prodigy, he entered Yale College at 13 and graduated four years later as class valedictorian at

---

[40] Wesley, vol. 1, 426-27, Sept. 6, 1742.
[41] Wesley, vol. 2 of *The Works of John Wesley*, 429.

the age of 17. He was a diligent student of Scripture, and became versed in the ancient languages and prepared himself thoroughly for the service of the Lord.

In 1729, Edwards became pastor of the Congregational Church, Northampton, Massachusetts. There he continued his discipline, diligently studying for 13 hours each day, while also spending much time in prayer. During this period, he became very concerned by what he described as the "spiritual deadness" throughout the land, and consequently he set himself to pray for a "revival of religion."

Spiritual awakening began to grip entire towns along the eastern seaboard. In Northampton, Edwards said that an awesome sense of God's presence seemed to permeate the entire community. Without any kind of evangelistic outreach or special meetings, "souls did as it were come by flocks to Jesus Christ."[42] In every part of town, the Spirit of God was powerfully at work until "there was scarcely a single person in the town, old or young, left unconcerned about the great things of the eternal world."[43] According to Edwards, God made a "glorious alteration in the town . . . and the town seemed to be full of the presence of God."[44]

---

[42] Edwards, "A Narrative of Surprising Conversions," *Jonathan Edwards on Revival* (Carlisle, PA: Banner of Truth Trust, 1994), 13.

[43] Edwards, 13.

[44] Edwards, 14.

Similar scenes occurred in towns and cities along the eastern seaboard. Philadelphia experienced such a transformation that it amazed Benjamin Franklin, one of America's Founding Fathers. Franklin, a printer in Philadelphia did not profess to be a Christian, but he recognized and described this amazing transformation in his autobiography.

> From being thoughtless or indifferent about religion, it seemed as if all the world were growing religious so that one could not walk through the town in an evening without hearing psalms sung in different families of every street.[45]

The Great Awakening grew out of prayer and the preaching of Biblical truth. In fact, Edwards writes that the revival brought a new love and appreciation for the Scriptures.

> While God was so remarkably amongst us by His Spirit, there was no book so delightful as the Bible; especially the book of Psalms, the Prophecy of Isaiah, and the New Testament. Some, by reason of their love to God's word, at times have been wonderfully delighted and affected at the sight of a Bible.[46]

According to Edwards, an important sign that a revival is from God is that people are stirred to a greater love and respect for the Word of God. On the

---

[45] Hyatt, *2000 Years of Charismatic Christianity*, 2002, 118.

[46] Edwards, "A Narrative of Surprising Conversions," 47.

other hand, Edwards said that if a revival does not provoke in people a hunger and desire for God's Word, it is a sign that something is amiss.

Charles Finney and Revival in 19th Century America

The 19th Century was a time of great spiritual awakening in America. The Second Great Awakening (1790–1840s), the 1857-58 Prayer Revival, and the revivals led by Charles G. Finney are the best known.

Finney (1792-1875) was converted at the age of 29 while practicing law in Upstate New York. From the moment of his conversion, he knew he was called to preach, and he gave himself totally to that endeavor. This meant becoming a diligent student of Scripture, to which he gave himself unreservedly throughout the remainder of his life. In his *Autobiography*, he recalls an experience he had many years after his conversion, while conducting a meeting in Boston:

> After the evening services, I would retire as early as I well could; but rose at four o'clock in the morning, because I could sleep no longer, and immediately went to the study, and became engaged in prayer. My days were spent, so far as I could get time, in searching the Scriptures; I read nothing all that winter but my Bible; and a great deal of it seemed new to me.[47]

---

[47] Edman, *Finney Lives On*, 58.

Finney's meetings in Rochester, New York, lasted for six months, resulting in thousands of conversions and the transformation of that city. One of the converts, Charles P. Bush, became a leading pastor in New York City and recalled the impact of the revival.

> The whole community was stirred. Religion was the topic of conversation in the house, in the shop, in the office, and on the street. The only theater in the city was converted into a livery stable; the only circus into a soap and candle factory. Grog shops [bars] were closed; the Sabbath was honored; the sanctuaries were thronged with happy worshippers; a new impulse was given to every philanthropic enterprise; the fountains of benevolence opened, and men lived to do good.[48]

For Finney, the evidence of revival was that of changed lives, rather than that of outward excitement or manifestations. In fact, Finney discouraged extreme outward displays of emotion. During a revival in Rome, New York, he tells of one meeting in which, toward the end, he sensed that the congregation was on the brink of "an outburst of feeling that would be almost uncontrollable." He said,

> The agitation deepened every moment; and as I could hear their sobs and sighs, I closed my prayer and rose suddenly from my knees. They all arose, and I said, "Now please go

---

[48] Edman, *Finney Lives On*, 68.

home without speaking a word to each other. Try to keep silent, and do not break out into any boisterous manifestation of feeling; but go without saying a word to your rooms."[49]

As they were leaving, a young man no longer able to stand, fell on his companions, causing them all to fall under the power of God. Many revivalists today, because of identifying revival with outward excitement, would have seen this as an opportunity to whip the meeting into a frenzy. But Finney, in his wisdom, quieted them and did not allow the outward manifestations to go any further. He said,

> This had well nigh produced a loud shrieking; but I hushed them down and said to the young men, "Please set that door wide open and go out and let all retire in silence." They did as I requested. They did not shriek; but they went out sobbing and sighing, and their sobs and sighs could be heard till they got out into the street.[50]

The people went home with pent-up emotions stirred in them by the Word and Spirit of God. One man, as soon as he stepped inside his home, fell to the floor weeping and crying out to God for mercy. In awe, his wife and children gathered round him and were subsequently converted to Christ. Similar scenes took place in homes throughout the city that

---

[49] Charles G. Finney, *An Autobiography*, (Old Tappan, NJ: Fleming H. Revell, 1908), 161.

[50] Finney, *An Autobiography*, 162.

night and continued into the following day. *Revival Fire* had come to the city of Rome, NY.

A Question to Consider

These revivals amaze us. Equally amazing to us may be that God affected such significant change without the religious ways and means that we tend to employ today. They had no praise bands or worship teams. They did not give altar calls or have prayer lines. They did not practice spiritual warfare or mapping. They had no self-appointed apostles or prophets. Yet God instigated revival beyond anything we have seen in our generation. Is it possible that they were more Biblical in their approach than we have been in our efforts? Is it possible that we need to be more discerning and to think more Biblically about revival?

We frequently have religious excitements and enthusiasm gotten up by the cunning methods and hypnotic influence of the mere professional evangelist or "revivalist," but these are not Revivals, and are not needed: they are a curse and not a blessing; they are the devil's imitation of a Revival.

R. A. Torrey

Chapter 11

THE EMERGENCE OF THE PROFESSIONAL REVIVALIST

"The most fundamental trouble with most of our present-day, so-called revivals is, that they are man-made and not God sent. They are worked up (I almost said faked up) by man's cunningly devised machinery—not prayed down." - *R. A. Torrey*

Prior to the 19th Century, the word "revival" was rarely used, and when it was used, it normally referred to the revitalization of one's personal faith in Jesus or the revitalization of the faith of a church or a community. These revivals, as we call them, were usually led by ministers, such as Wesley, Edwards, and Whitefield, who, from their diligent search of Scripture, saw that the church of their day had veered from the Biblical pattern. To remedy the situation, they did not seek or pursue something called "revival." Instead, they sought to recover the faith and dynamism of New Testament Christianity. They did not consider themselves "revivalists," but merely ministers of the gospel seeking to preach and practice New Testament Christianity.

Charles Finney Confronts Hyper-Calvinism.

A shift began with Charles Finney, who faced the

deadening tenets of the hyper-Calvinism permeating the 19th Century American church. Hyper-Calvinism is a theological system that emphasizes the sovereignty of God to the extreme, purporting that God has already determined from all eternity who will be saved and who will be damned. Finney tells how pastors of his day would tell concerned inquirers to go home and pray and read their Bible, and if they were one of the elect they would be saved, but if they were not one of the elect, there was nothing anyone could do. In this system of thought, revival was seen as a sovereign work of God totally separate from any human means or instrumentality.

Finney responded by rightfully emphasizing human responsibility in salvation and in all relations with God. He denied that humanity was unable to respond to the demands of the Gospel, as the hyper-Calvinists taught, and he provoked much opposition and controversy when he began calling on those to stand who were ready to submit their lives to the claims of Christ. Trained as a lawyer, he considered himself called to argue God's case before an unbelieving world. His messages, very logical and backed by much prayer, powerfully impacted his audiences.

In reaction to the Calvinistic notion that a revival is entirely a sovereign work of God, Finney, in the early days of his ministry, declared that a revival was no more a miracle than a crop of wheat. He pointed out that if a farmer used the proper means, including plowing, planting, and watering, then his desire for a harvest would be realized. For a farmer to pray for a harvest without using the proper means would be foolish. In the same way, argued Finney, revival will always occur when the proper means are employed. He thus made revival an objective and goal to be sought and obtained by using the proper means.

The Shift to the Other Extreme

The means Finney emphasized for a revival were private and public prayer, protracted meetings, pointed preaching, and personal witnessing. He was probably the first to use the word "revival" on a regular basis and as an objective that Christians should pursue. In this sense, Finney became the first professional evangelist or revivalist. Producing revival was his vocation. Other revivalists, lacking his gifts and commitment to truth, soon followed suit.

Finney's emphasis on human responsibility opened the door for revival to be seen as a human enterprise. As others picked up his concepts and ran with them, God's sovereign grace and choice in pouring out His Spirit was diminished, and human responsibility and ability to create "revival" were highlighted.

This opened the door for all sorts of questionable means being employed to produce revival. Since the success of the professional revivalist hinged on human ability to create an emotional and exciting religious event, revivals became increasingly shallow. Instead of being the result of the Holy Spirit's working through the Word of God to convict and to change lives, "revivals" often were simply the creation of individuals who were adept at stirring and manipulating people's emotions. In other words, "strange fire" was brought into the sanctuary of God in the name of "revival."

R. A. Torrey, (1856-1928), an associate of D. L. Moody (1837-1899) and a successful revivalist himself, came on the scene a generation after Finney. He lamented,

> We frequently have religious excitements and enthusiasms gotten up by the cunning methods and hypnotic influence of the mere professional evangelist or "revivalist," but these are not Revivals, and are not needed: they are a curse and not a blessing; they are the devil's imitations of a Revival.[51]

Biblical Revival Yields to the Sovereignty of God.

Biblical revival is a co-operation between the human and the Divine. In his later years, Finney acknowledged that he had put too much emphasis on human ability to produce revival. This had led to the erroneous notion that by employing certain means, one could produce a revival at the time and place of his choosing. Finney, in fact, saw so many people "backslide from a revival state," that he began to question if there was not something higher and more stable that Christians should pursue.[52]

The "backsliding," Finney observed, was the bad

---

[51] R. A. Torrey, *The Power of Prayer and the Prayer of Power* (Grand Rapids: Zondervan, 1924), 228.

[52] Finney, *An Autobiography,* 340.

fruit of making "revival" an end or goal to be obtained. The only legitimate end or goal for every Christian is Jesus Christ and conformity to His will. Romans 8:29 says, *For whom He did foreknow, he also predestined to be conformed to the image of His Son.* Genuine, heaven-sent revival will always have Jesus Christ as its end or goal. If revival itself becomes the end, then bad fruit, as Finney discovered, will be the result.

Professional Revivalism in the 21st Century

Professional revivalism may be a greater problem in our century than it was in previous times. This is because the hyper-Arminian mindset (overemphasizing human ability) that emerged out of Finney's theology has been coupled with the influences of an entertainment-driven culture and a personal success orientation. As a result, little value is placed on repentance, prayer, and waiting on God for a sovereign outpouring of the Holy Spirit. Instead, attention is given to what can be done on a human level to draw crowds and stir excitement. Challenging us regarding this, Duncan Campbell (1898-1972), the Welsh preacher whom God used in the mighty revival on the Hebrides Islands (1949-1952), writes,

> We have seen crowded churches. We have seen many professions. We have seen hundreds, yes, and thousands responding to what you speak of here as the altar call. But, I want to say this, dear people, and I say it without fear of contradiction, that you can have all that . . . without God! Now, that may startle you, but I say again, you

can have all that . . . on mere human levels.[53]

In the sort of ego-centric milieu that has emerged in American Christianity, revival too often is the product of a charismatic leader who knows how to control a crowd and generate excitement. Exaggerated claims, manipulative sermons, and flamboyant antics are used to stir the emotions of the masses and create a "revival." In such an event, the Word of God is preempted by Christian entertainment or by testimonies of exciting "spiritual" experiences.

This approach, coupled with the neglect of Scripture, has dire consequences. "Strange fire" inevitably becomes a part of the mix. Individual casualties and tragedy are commonly the result. Such revivals tend either to drag on in pursuit of increasingly bizarre practices or to collapse under the weight of their own sin and neglect of Biblical truth.

What, then, is the safeguard? In our day, we must reclaim the Word of God as central in all we say and do. This generation desperately needs to see the power and purity of a Biblical Revival. Torrey's comment about the state of revivalism in his day rings true for the 21st century Church.

> The most fundamental trouble with most of our present-day, so called revivals is, that they are man-made and not God sent. They are worked up (I almost said faked up) by man's cunningly devised machinery—not

---

[53] Duncan Campbell, *The Nature of A God Sent Revival* (Euless, TX: Successful Christian Living Ministries, n.d.) 11-12.

prayed down.[54]

Our God is the sovereign Lord, not only of this universe, but also of revival. If the Church in Finney's day was guilty of not taking their responsibility for revival, the modern charismatic church has gone to the other extreme and made revival a mere human enterprise. It is time for the North American church to repent of this sin and be converted *that times of refreshing may come from the presence of the Lord* (Acts 3:19). It is time for genuine *Revival Fire*.

---

[54] Torrey, *The Power of Prayer and the Prayer of Power*, 62.

The fact is that we will not quench the Holy Spirit by doing what He has commanded us to do, *i.e.,* test the spirits (1 John 4:1-6). We may quench spiritual pride and religious ambition, but not the Holy Spirit. Joseph Smith and the early Mormons did not test the spirits, nor did they judge their prophetic words and supernatural experiences by the canon or rule of Scripture. Instead they twisted Scripture to make it fit their experience. Let us avoid this at all costs.

Chapter 12

THE TRAGEDY OF REVIVAL WITHOUT THE BIBLE

Try all things by the written word, and let all bow down before it. You're in danger of enthusiasm every hour, if you depart ever so little from the Scripture: yea; from that plain, literal meaning of any text, taken with the context. *– John Wesley*

When revival and the supernatural are pursued without a corresponding commitment to Biblical truth, the pursuer opens himself or herself to deceiving spirits, referred to in Scripture as *angels of light* (II Corinthians 11:14). For example, the early Mormons pursued sensational, spiritual phenomena and experienced speaking in tongues, prophecy, falling under the power, visions, and angelic visitations. This heretical movement actually emerged out of the Second Great Awakening, one of the most powerful revivals in Christian history. In fact, an examination of the beginnings of Mormonism reveals many similarities with the present day revival-prophetic movement. Their example is a wake-up call for all who embrace the supernatural ministry of the Holy Spirit to be diligent in carrying out the Biblical commands to test the spirits and to judge prophetic and supernatural manifestations. After all, Satan, the deceiver, does not come in a red suit with horns and a pitchfork, but as an *angel of light*.

Peter Cartwright's Autobiography

Peter Cartwright (1785-1872) was a circuit-riding, Methodist preacher and one of the most famous revivalists of the Second Great Awakening. His autobiography offers intriguing reading and provides valuable information concerning the religious landscape in early and mid-19th Century America.

His autobiography also offers a personal glimpse into the origins of Mormonism and how it began in the milieu of religious revivalism. His account provides an historical example of the dangers of naively embracing everything sensational and of the importance of following the example of the Bereans who, *Searched the Scriptures daily to find out whether these things were so* (Acts 17:11).

The Mormons Speak in Tongues

Cartwright tells about a particular camp meeting he was conducting in which a certain group remained behind at the end of one of the services, singing and praising God. Eventually, one of the women began to shout and then "swooned away," falling into her husband's arms where she lay, as if in a trance. Her husband announced that she was, indeed, in a trance and that when she came out of it, she would speak in an unknown language that he would interpret. This was obviously not something new for them.

By this time, a large, curious crowd had gathered. Cartwright, believing they were merely drawing attention to themselves, decided to break up their meeting. As he walked into the midst of the group, the woman in the trance suddenly opened her eyes, laid her hand on his arm, and said,

"Dear friend, I have a message directly from God to you." Cartwright, who was a gruff sort of person, said,

"I stopped her short and said, 'I will have none of your message.'" The woman's husband, who was to interpret the message, angrily replied,

"Sir this is my wife, and I will defend her at the risk of my life." Cartwright retorted,

"Sir, this is my camp meeting, and I will maintain the good order of it at the risk of my life."

After an exchange of emotionally charged words, the group finally left. Cartwright identified them as Mormons, followers of a "Joe Smith" with whom he had had several conversations.

Cartwright Meets Joe Smith.

Cartwright tells about Joe Smith sharing with him his vision for the restoration of the New Testament church. According to Smith, during a time of prayer in Upstate New York, he had inquired about which church was the right one. Smith said,

I saw a pillar of light exactly over my head, above the brightness of the sun, which descended gradually until it fell upon me. When the light rested upon me I saw two Personages, whose brightness and glory defy all description, standing above me in the air.[55]

According to Smith, one of the "personages" called him by name and said, pointing to the other, "This is My Beloved Son. Hear Him."

In Smith's own account there is no indication that he fell on his face in awe and worship. Instead, he seemed to take it all in stride and had the presence of mind to ask which church was right and which he should join. The answer, according to Smith, was that "they were all wrong."

Cartwright says that Smith told him that, of all the churches then in existence, the Methodist church was the closest to the church of the New Testament,

"But they had stopped short by not claiming the gift of tongues, of prophecy, and of miracles." He went on to tell Cartwright,

> If you will go with me to Nauvoo [an early Mormon community], I will show you many living witnesses that will testify that they were, by the saints, cured of blindness, lameness, deafness, dumbness, and all the diseases that human flesh is heir to. And I will show you that we have the gift of tongues, and can speak in unknown languages, and that the saints can drink any deadly poison and it will not hurt them.[56]

---

[55] Ruth Tucker, *Another Gospel* (Grand Rapids: Zondervan, 2004), 51.

[56] Peter Cartwright, "Wrestling with God and Man," *Christian History*, issue 45 (vol. XIV, no. 1), 20.

Visions and Angelic Visitations

Joseph Smith and his early followers not only claimed the miraculous gifts of the Spirit, but they also claimed to experience visions and angelic visitations on a regular basis. This being the case, it is likely that those of the contemporary prophetic movement would likely have designated Smith as a prophet or seer, had they been there.

On one occasion, according to Smith, an angel named Moroni appeared to him and told him where to find the plates on which were inscribed the Book of Mormon, written in an ancient Egyptian text. Smith claimed that, while he and an associate, Oliver Cowdery, were translating the book, John the Baptist, as well as Peter, James, and John, appeared to them and ordained them to the priesthood of Melchizedek. (Demons always play on human pride, telling us how important we will be if we accept the revelation they bring.)

Smith Proves to be Angry and Unteachable.

In his meeting with Smith, Cartwright began to question him about his doctrine. As he proceeded, it soon became obvious that Smith had left behind Biblical truth and was following sensational teachings based on prophecies, and purported visions, and angelic visitations. As Cartwright continued pointing out his error from Scripture, he said that Smith's "wrath boiled over" and "he cursed me in the name of his God." Smith angrily retorted,

I will show you sir, that I will raise up a government in these United States which will overturn the present government, and I will raise up a new religion that will overturn every other form of religion in this country.[57]

The Dedication of the First Mormon Temple

In 1831, based on an alleged revelation from God, Smith and many of his followers migrated to Kirkland, Ohio. There they built and dedicated the first Mormon temple in 1836. According to one Mormon historian, they experienced a spiritual outpouring possibly unmatched in church history. Smith himself wrote a detailed description.

A noise was heard like the sound of a rushing mighty wind, which filled the Temple, and all the congregation simultaneously arose, being moved upon by an invisible power; many began to speak in tongues and prophesy; others saw glorious visions; and I beheld the Temple filled with angels, which fact I declared to the congregation. The people of the neighborhood came running (hearing an unusual sound within, and seeing a bright light like a pillar of fire resting on the Temple), and were astonished at what was taking place. This continued until the meeting closed at eleven P.M.[58]

---

[57] Cartwright, "Wrestling With God and Man," 21.

[58] Tucker, *Another Gospel*, 61.

What Can We Learn from Mormonism?

Out of this movement that based its beliefs on prophecies, visions, and angelic visitations, has grown a movement that today numbers millions of followers around the world. While many of their beliefs are obviously Christian in origin, they also hold to many beliefs that have no basis in Scripture and that are at odds with Biblical Christianity. This happened because they exalted their experiences and writings, such as the Book of Mormon, to equal status with the Bible. In doing so, they allowed "strange fire" into their midst.

The following suggestions can help us avoid repeating the mistakes made by this movement.

SUGGESTION 1:
Make the Diligent Study of
God's Word the Number 1 Priority.

Anything can be proven by a technique known as proof-texting (*i.e.,* quoting verses out of context), but the Bereans provide a good example of the proper approach (Acts 17:11). They were commended because, instead of naively accepting what Paul and Silas preached, *they searched the Scriptures daily to find out whether those things were so.* This approach provides protection and guidance for those of us today who value the experiences that revival brings. Let's follow the Berean example!

Do Not Be Afraid to "Test the Spirits."

The fact is that we will not quench the Holy Spirit by doing what He has commanded us to do (1 John 4:1-6). We may quench spiritual pride and religious ambition, but not the Holy Spirit. Joseph Smith and the early Mormons did not test the spirits, nor did they judge their prophetic words and supernatural experiences by the canon or rule of Scripture. Instead they twisted Scripture to make it fit their experience. Let's avoid this at all costs.

SUGGESTION 3:
Do Not Chase the Sensational.

It is dangerous to try to make the supernatural happen. Manifestations of the Spirit occur as the Spirit wills, not as we will (I Corinthians 12:11). Signs are to follow the believer and the preaching of the Word, not the reverse. We should simply be sensitive to and obedient to the leading of the Holy Spirit. The early Mormons pursued visions, angels, and so on—and this led to departure from Biblical truth. If we would be wise, we would stay with Scripture and exercise common sense, which the Bible calls "wisdom."

SUGGESTION 4:
Avoid Spiritual Pride.

God has not called us to be important, but simply obedient. We can rest in the fact that each of us is so important to God that He came in the Person of Jesus

Christ and died for us that we might know Him and live with Him forever. But fallen human nature drives people to strive for importance. This was apparent in Joseph Smith's remark to Peter Cartwright, that if Cartwright would join him,

"We could sweep, not only the Methodist church, but all the churches, and you would be looked up to as one of the Lord's greatest prophets."[59]

Do you see and hear the pride in that statement? It behooves us to remember that "the stronghold of deception is pride."

SUGGESTION 5:
Avoid an Elitist Mindset.

Smith claimed that he and his followers were the true, restored church of the New Testament and that all other churches were false churches. Mormons still believe this. This error is based in pride and perhaps in an unhealthy need to feel important, significant, and powerful.

Love the Truth.

Mormonism is an obvious, historical example of what can happen when people seek revival or spiritual experiences apart from Biblical truth. The Written Word of God must be the ultimate standard. II Thessalonians speaks of a great deception in the last days and says it will happen to those who *did not receive the love of the truth, that they might be saved* (II

---

[59] Cartwright, "Wrestling with God and Man," 20.

Thessalonians 2:10). We are to love and pursue the truth. We are to love truth more than anything the world or the devil would offer, including success, popularity, and riches. Truth is found in God's Word. Regarding this, Jesus prayed for His disciples, *Sanctify them by Your truth. Your word is truth* (John 17:17). Only with a 100% love and commitment to truth will we be protected from the great deception of the last days. Jesus said it like this,

> *If you abide in My word, you are My disciples indeed. And you shall know the truth, and the truth shall make you free* (John 8:31-32).

Chapter 13

SPIRITUAL MANIFESTATIONS – A BIBLICAL PERSPECTIVE

"I think it is tempting God to require such signs. That there is something of God in it, I doubt not. But the devil, I believe, does interpose. I think it will encourage the French Prophets, take people away from the written word, and make them depend on visions, convulsions, etc., more than on the promises and precepts of the gospel." - *George Whitfield*

Revivals have always been accompanied by unique, and sometimes bizarre, manifestations among its participants. The most common of these have been falling, weeping, shouting, laughing, crying out, shaking, and so on. These manifestations have always been controversial, with the most common criticism being that they are disorderly, fleshly, and perhaps even demonic. However, supporters of these manifestations identify them as signs of God's presence in the midst of His people. How, then, can we distinguish that which is truly of God?

The need is to be open without being naive and to be critical without being judgmental. In this process, Scripture provides the ultimate standard by which such manifestations are evaluated. It is also helpful to consider two categories of manifestations: cultural manifestations and supernatural manifestations.

Emotional and physical reactions should be expected responses from people who are experiencing the Holy Spirit's power. This is especially true if it is a person's first encounter with God's manifest presence. Many times, people do not know how to respond, and depending on the measure of the Spirit they are experiencing, they may exhibit bizarre behavior or act in strange ways. Just as much pain, joy, and commotion accompanies the birth of a baby in the natural realm, so it is when there is "life again" or revival in the Church. But just as it is normal for the climate to shift to one of tranquility, love, and quiet joy after the birth, so it is normal in revival for a calm to settle the heart of the individual and congregation after the initial shock and novelty of revival. John Wesley said,

> I have generally observed more or less of these outward symptoms (falling, shaking, convulsing, shouting, etc.) to attend the beginning of a general work of God: So it was in New England, Scotland, Holland, Ireland, and many parts of England; but after a time they gradually decrease, and the work goes on more quietly and silently. Those whom it pleases God to employ in His work, ought to be quite passive in this respect: They should choose nothing, but leave entirely to him all the circumstances of his own work.[60]

The problem has been that revival leaders have

---

[60] Wesley, vol. 2 of *The Works of John Wesley*, 510.

too often equated manifestations with revival and have attempted to keep the manifestations going apart from the Holy Spirit. This then leads to "fleshly" manifestations and "strange fire" being offered in the place of genuine *Revival Fire*. A mild example of this was expressed by an African student in a class I was teaching. Placing his hand on his forehead and pushing his head backward, he exclaimed,

"Why do American preachers push you to the floor?"

Manifestations as Cultural Expressions

Growing up in a Pentecostal church that valued spiritual manifestations, I learned very early that there is a cultural aspect to people's response to the Holy Spirit. In our Assembly of God, people would commonly "shout" when there was "a move of the Spirit." These shouts of praise might be accompanied by jumping, jerking, and dancing exuberantly.

As a young man, I began playing lead guitar with a Church of God (Cleveland, TN) singing group and found myself in congregations belonging to that denomination. Immediately, I noticed that the Church of God people responded differently to the Holy Spirit's presence than did those of the Assemblies of God. I particularly noticed that the Church of God women, when prayed for by the laying on of hands, would arch their backs in a certain, peculiar way. I noticed the young girls responding exactly the same way. Even as a young believer, it became obvious to me that the unique responses of both groups were learned behaviors.

This is not to say that they were not experiencing God's presence, but to point out that they had learned certain ways to respond to God's presence that were unique to their church cultures. Since that time, I have repeatedly seen this feature in revivals, where certain outward expressions or behavior become esteemed and valued in that revival. People who embrace the revival seem to learn by osmosis how they are expected to respond to the Spirit's presence. Within the revival, these cultural manifestations are usually looked upon as the direct activity of the Holy Spirit and signs of His presence.

Unfortunately, these manifestations often become marks of spirituality and those who do not exhibit the same sort of behavior are looked down upon. Much pressure is placed on individuals to act a certain way if they want to be esteemed as "spiritual" and accepted into the "tribe." Some will then begin to exhibit such behavior of their own initiative, apart from the Holy Spirit. This may take the form of falling when prayed for, jerking in a particular manner, producing a grunting sound, or making some other physical expression.

I have ministered in churches where it was obvious that people had been trained—probably subtly—to fall when prayed for. I remember one man looking behind him to make sure the catcher was there before he fell backward as I prayed for him.

Let's learn to discern between Spirit and culture,

and between the human soul and spirit.

The Difference between Soul and Spirit

To discern between soul and spirit is helpful in recognizing the source of an outward manifestation. Is a behavior a response to the Spirit of God or is it merely a human or fleshy display? The New Testament teaches that there is a difference between the human soul and the human spirit. In I Thessalonians 5:23, for example, Paul says, *May your whole spirit, soul, and body be preserved blameless at the coming of our Lord Jesus Christ.* Hebrews 14:12 clearly says that the soul and spirit are two distinct entities and that only the Word of God can divide the two. Making a distinction between soul and spirit can be very helpful in discerning the source of a manifestation.

The spirit is the innermost part of our being and is that part that is regenerated when we are born again. It is through our human spirit that we have an awareness of God and the spirit realm. In born-again believers, the spirit is the place where the Holy Spirit dwells and, therefore, the place from which gifts of the Holy Spirit flow. Our spirit is sometimes referred to in Scripture as "the heart." For example, Jesus was speaking of the human spirit when He said, *He who believes on Me, as the Scripture has said, out of his heart will flow rivers of living water* (John 7:38).

The soul, on the other hand, consists of our mind, will, and emotions. It is the seat of the personality—the ego—and is that part of our being that gives us self-awareness. The soul, *i.e.*, mind, will, and emotions, can be moved by a variety of outward stimuli. Good music, for example, has the power to stir positive emotions of love, nostalgia, and compassion apart from the Holy Spirit. Likewise, a gifted orator can stir emotions and move people to behave in ways they otherwise would not. These are mere feelings of the soul and have nothing to do with the Holy Spirit. This is what John Wesley was referring to when, on October 29, 1762, he cautioned a colleague who was mistaking his own thoughts and imaginations for the Holy Spirit. Wesley said:

> I dislike something that has the appearance of enthusiasm, overvaluing feelings and inward impressions; mistaking the mere work of imagination for the voice of the Spirit, and undervaluing reason, knowledge, and wisdom in general.[61]

We have the same obligation today to distinguish between the soul and spirit in ourselves and in others.

Discerning Between Soul & Spirit

I recall visiting a revival meeting where there were many outward manifestations—laughing, falling, and so on—and I left the meeting with an inward sense of edification and refreshing. Later, I visited another revival where the same manifestations were occurring, and even though people were laughing, falling, and shouting in similar ways, I left this meeting grieved and troubled inside. The difference was

---

[61] Wesley, vol. 3 of *The Works of John Wesley*, 98.

that the manifestations in the first revival were, for the most part, honest responses to the Spirit's presence. In the second venue, where my spirit was grieved, the manifestations originated in the soul, for the most part. They were not responses to the Holy Spirit, but tended, instead, to be worked up religious frenzy.

Learning to distinguish between soul and spirit also has an incredible bearing on the operation of the gift of prophecy. I recall a "prophet" once giving me a prophetic word about my "little brother" about whom he said I had been very concerned. He claimed that God had just revealed to him that there was no need for my concern, for my little brother would be saved. Now, there was only one problem with this prophecy: I do not have a little brother!

When I shared this fact with the prophet he seemed to be embarrassed and replied,

"I will have to be more careful."

He was not a false prophet, but simply an individual who had never learned to distinguish between his soul and spirit. The prophecy was neither from God nor the devil, but had been formulated in his soul, (i.e., his mind will and emotions), perhaps motivated by a need for attention or importance. This is why I Thessalonians 5:21 says, *Test all things; hold fast what is good.*

Supernatural Manifestations

In 1980, Sue and I saw a powerful move of the Holy Spirit in Saint John, New Brunswick, where we were planting a congregation and ministry. When this outpouring of the Holy Spirit came, people began to fall—but not backward. They were falling forward. One man later admitted that he, at first, thought something was amiss because he had never known of anyone falling forward. This manifestation continued for a time and then gradually ceased, and we did not try to keep it happening. These were supernatural occurrences and not cultural responses, for no one there had ever seen or experienced this before.

Supernatural manifestations, assuming they are from God, are those that are a direct result of the activity of the Holy Spirit in or upon a person. A Biblical example would be Paul falling to the ground and being blinded by an incredibly bright light when he encountered the Risen Lord Jesus on the road from Jerusalem to Damascus. This was no cultural response to God's presence; this was Paul being directly impacted by God's presence and power. Another example would be Peter falling into a trance and seeing a vision of a sheet with all kinds of unclean animals being let down from heaven and then hearing a voice saying, "Arise Peter, kill and eat." As with Paul on the Damascus Road, this was not a cultural response on Peter's part. It was the direct work of the Holy Spirit in his life. Supernatural manifestations would also include the supernatural healings and miracles that are recorded in the Gospels and Acts.

Supernatural manifestations may also be initiated by Satan. A young slave girl, possessed with a false prophetic spirit, followed Paul and Silas for many days proclaiming, *These men are servants of the Most*

High God, who proclaim to us the way of salvation (Acts 16:17). What she said was true and flattering, but it was not from God. Paul recognized that an evil spirit was behind the words and cast it out. Paul warns that the coming of the anti-Christ will be *with all power, signs, and lying wonders* (I Thessalonians 2:9). This is why the New Testament is filled with warnings and admonitions to test the spirits and to judge or evaluate spiritual manifestations and prophetic utterances (I John 4:1).

Guidelines Concerning Manifestations

SUGGESTION 1:
Be Open to Manifestations without Being Naïve.

People must have the freedom to respond with integrity—and with even intensity—to the Spirit of the Lord and to express their hearts to Him in praise and worship. We must not, however, assume that every shout or every dance or every "thus saith the Lord" is, in fact, from God. Wise leaders, without tolerating fleshly disorder, will leave room for unique expressions with different personalities and within different cultures.

SUGGESTION 2:
Do Not Think that Manifestations Equal Revival.

Powerful works of grace can occur in people's hearts apart from outward displays and manifestations. In the Second Great Awakening early in the 19th Century, for example, the revivals at Yale under President Timothy

Dwight, grandson of Jonathan Edwards, were almost entirely without outward manifestation. The Spirit of God came as the dew from heaven, quiet, gentle, and not observed by eye nor felt by hand, but hearts were melted before God and tears of penitence flowed silently.[62] The college and the community were transformed. It was genuine *Revival Fire*.

SUGGESTION 3:

Seek the Lord, Not Manifestations.

A woman approached William Seymour at Azusa Street, imploring him to "pray for me that I will get the tongues." Seymour replied,

"Now, see here, Sister Sadie, don't you go seeking tongues. You seek Jesus. He's the One."

SUGGESTION 4:

Do Not Allow Manifestations to Preempt the Centrality of Christ and the Preaching of the Word of God.

We must not fall in love with manifestations, running here and there in pursuit of the most exciting antics on display or of a place where we can experience the biggest goose bumps. Instead, we are to keep our eyes on Jesus, focusing our attention on building our faith in His Word. Believers are not to follow signs; signs are to follow believers and the preaching of the Word. We are to walk by faith, not by sight, *i.e.,* not by outward manifestations.

---

[62] Edman, *Finney Lives On*, 162

Chapter 14

BIBLICAL LEADERSHIP
FOR BIBLICAL REVIVAL

"In matters of religion, I regard no writings but the inspired [Scripture]. Tauler, Behmen, and a whole army of mystic authors are with me nothing to St. Paul. In every point I appeal "to the law and the testimony," and value no authority but this." - *John Wesley*

If we are to see genuine *Revival Fire* in this generation, we must have the kind of godly leadership that can nurture and guide such revival. It is important, therefore, to distinguish between leadership that is traditional and institutional in character, and leadership that is in line with the Biblical model.

- Traditional, institutional leadership tends to quench revival fire; whereas, the Biblical model of leadership will guide and facilitate genuine revival.

- Traditional, institutional leadership feels a need to be in control; whereas, the Biblical model is willing to surrender control to the Holy Spirit while exercising responsible influence over what is happening.

- Traditional, institutional leadership uses others for its own benefit; whereas, the Biblical model empowers others.

- Traditional, institutional leadership tends to dominate; whereas, the Biblical model facilitates.

- Traditional, institutional leadership attracts and holds on to followers; whereas, Biblical leadership develops and releases leaders.

The following are five characteristics of Biblical leadership that will help to facilitate and nurture genuine, Heaven-sent *Revival Fire*.

CHARACTERISTIC 1:
Biblical Leadership Is Rooted in Serving.

Jesus presented this revolutionary model of leadership to The Twelve in Matthew 20:25-26 when they were vying for what they thought would be positions of authority in His kingdom. Jesus reproved them for thinking like the Gentiles, *i.e.*, like those who do not know God. He says,

> *You know that the rulers (i.e., archontes) of the Gentiles lord it over them, and those who are great exercise authority over them. Yet it shall not be so among you; but whoever desires to become great among you, let him be your servant (i.e., diakonos).*

In this scenario, Jesus recognizes two possible models of leadership; the *archon* model, which is that of the world, and the *diakonos* model, which is the kind that is to characterize His followers. An *archon* was a ruler whose leadership was characterized by power and control. In the New Testament, this word is used of secular rulers, but never of Christian leaders. Jesus says here that the *archon* model of leadership is not acceptable in His kingdom.

In sharp contrast to the *archon* was the *diakonos*, a household servant who carried out the mundane tasks and the desires of the master or mistress of the house. *Thayer's Greek-English Lexicon* defines a *diakonos* as "one who executes the commands of another" and one who advances others' interests even at the sacrifice of that person's own interests. In other words, neither pre-eminence nor prestige is associated with the word *diakonos*. Rather, the word describes a person who renders lowly service on behalf of others. Jesus said that this *diakonos* model of leadership is the kind that characterizes His kingdom.

Diakonos is Paul's favorite word to describe his own ministry. He uses it more than any other word to describe himself. To the Corinthians, who were elevating Apollos and him to pedestals and forming cliques around them, he rhetorically asks, *Who then is Paul and who is Apollos, but servants (i.e., diakonoi) through whom you believed* (I Corinthians 3:5).

This shows that Paul understood his ministry in terms of responsibility and service, rather than in terms of office and power. Paul's understanding is characteristic of the entire New Testament. According to Kung,

> In the New Testament, not only is the word "hierarchy" consistently and deliberately avoided,

but so, too, are all secular words for "office" in connection with church functions, as they express a relationship of power. Instead of this, an all-encompassing term, *diakonia*, service (really "serving at table"), is used, which can nowhere evoke associations with any authority, control or position of dignity and power.[63]

Characteristic 2:
Biblical Leadership Is Based on Character and Calling.

Is it possible that some Christian leaders tend to derive their sense of security and status from an office they fill or a title they wear? If so, it is problematic because true Biblical leadership is rooted in the gift and commission given by God. It is separate, apart from, and different from any ecclesiastical office, position, or title. For this reason, when Christianity becomes institutionalized, one may occupy a church office and carry an ecclesiastical title without the gift and call from God.

Jesus did not carry a title to let people know He was the Messiah. In fact, when people recognized Him as the Messiah, He often instructed them not to tell anyone. He wanted people to follow Him because they had spiritual eyes to see Him for Who He was, not because He had captured their attention by a title, a unique way of dressing, or a particular ceremony.

---

[63] Kung, *Christianity: Essence, History and Future*, 321-22.

Words in the New Testament, such as *apostle, pastor, bishop, prophet,* and the like, were not words of office and title, but words that helped describe a person's function and responsibility. This is borne out by the fact that there is not one example of a New Testament leader being referred to with a title in front of his or her name.

That these words refer to function rather than to office is also borne out by the original meaning of the words. For example, the word "apostle" literally means "a sent one" and referred to someone who had received a specific commission from the Risen Lord to carry out a particular assignment. The word "pastor" is from the Greek word *poimen,* the word for "shepherd," and it is used as a metaphor highlighting the leader's responsibility to feed and care for the people, even as a shepherd feeds and cares for sheep. In a similar way, the word "bishop" is from the Greek word *episcopas,* which literally means to "watch over." Originally, it referred to anyone who had responsibility to "watch over" a situation; for example, a teacher in a classroom or a superintendent on a building project.

Paul borrowed *episcopas* from its popular Greek usage and used it to describe the responsibility of Christian leaders to watch over the affairs of a group of believers. The church father, Augustine, understood this original, functional meaning of *episcopas* and reminded his readers that the word refers to responsibility and not to authority. He then said,

"Therefore, he who loves to govern rather than do good is no bishop."[64]

Titles, if used at all, should be used to designate a leader's function and responsibility, not to give that person prestige and power over others. Along these lines, Jesus instructed His disciples not to use titles because they tend to elevate the one with the title over others, and all His followers are to be on the same level (Matthew 23:1-12).

CHARACTERISTIC 3:
Biblical Leadership Is *of* and *for* the People.

Christian leaders must realize that they exist for the people of God, and not the people for the leaders. This does not mean that leaders are subservient or subordinate to the people; rather, it means that they are responsible for equipping the people of God to become all that He created them to be. This is clearly borne out by a literal translation of Ephesians 4:12, where Paul says that God has set apostles, prophets, evangelists, pastors and teachers in the Church, *For the equipping of the saints for the work of the ministry for the building up of the body of Christ.*

The traditional translation of this passage makes it sound as though there are three purposes for each of these leadership gifts in the Church with each purpose preceded by the preposition "for." In Greek,

---

[64] P. Schaff and H. Wace, eds., vol. 2 of 15 vols., *Nicene and Post-Nicene Fathers of the Christian Church,* 1st series (Grand Rapids: Eerdmans, 1979), 413.

however, two different prepositions are used that indicate only one purpose for these leadership gifts.

- The first preposition is *pros* and precedes the phrase *the equipping of the saints*, which is the single purpose of these leadership gifts.
- The next two prepositions are both *eis*, which literally means "into."

Hence, a literal reading of this passage would be that God has set these leadership gifts in the church *For the equipping of the saints into the work of the ministry into the building up of the body of Christ.*

The word "equipping" in this verse is from the Greek word *katartismon*. It is the same word that Matthew used of the disciples when they had left their boats and were mending, tending to, or preparing their nets for the next fishing expedition (Matthew 4:21). The word *katartismon* means to "mend, heal, restore, equip, and prepare." Leadership gifts in the Church have this as their one purpose—to *katartismon* the saints so that the saints can then do the work of the ministry of building up the body of Christ.

Many New Testament scholars, therefore, see these leadership gifts, not as gifts that God gives to people, but as people whom God empowers and gives as gifts to His Church. They exist to equip and prepare the members of Christ's body to become all they were meant to be. Paul expressed this in writing to the Corinthians:

> *Therefore let no one boast in men. For all things are yours: whether Paul or Apollos or Cephas, or*

the world or life or death, or things present, or things to come—all are yours, And you are Christ's and Christ is God's (I Corinthians 3:21).

Biblical Leadership Is Gender Inclusive.

Several years ago, I received an email asking about the Greek word that is translated "men" in Ephesians 4:8. This person wanted to know if it was the plural form of *aner*, which refers to men as males, or if it was the plural form of *anthropos*, which is generic and includes both men and women. I was able to respond with the knowledge that it was, in fact, *anthropoi*, the plural form of *anthropos*, which means "people."

This is significant, being Paul's introduction to his discourse about what has been called "the 5-fold ministry" of apostle, prophet, evangelist, pastor and teacher. (Because the literary structure is unclear, some consider these four divisions instead of five, with pastor-teacher being considered one.) Regardless, had Paul wanted to restrict these leadership gifts to males, he could have used the plural form of *aner*. Instead, he used *anthropoi*, thereby embracing the fact that both men and women functioned in these leadership gifts and callings.

Paul makes the same point in his instructions to Timothy in II Timothy 2:2:

The things you have heard from me among many witnesses, commit these to faithful men (i.e., anthropoi, meaning "people") who will be able to teach others also.

Paul is telling Timothy to prepare for his departure from Ephesus by training leaders who will be able to take care of the believers in his absence. As in Ephesians 4:8, the word Paul uses is *anthropoi*, which is gender inclusive and clearly anticipates both men and women leaders in the church in Ephesus.

There are numerous examples in both the Old and New Testaments of women who functioned in leadership roles. The list includes, for example, Deborah, Huldah, and Miriam in the Old Testament. The list in the New Testament includes, for example, Junia, whom Paul, in Romans 16:7, recognized as an apostle. It also includes Phoebe, whom Paul, in Romans 16:2, referred to as *a helper of many and of myself also*. The Greek word translated "helper" in this verse is *prostates* and it literally means "to stand before." According to *Thayer's Greek-English Lexicon* it means "to set over, preside over, superintend, protect, and care for." The word obviously describes a function of leadership similar to that of a present day pastor who gives guidance and oversight to others. Paul says that Phoebe has been this to many, including himself.

It should be noted that all of these women are presented in Scripture in a positive light. Nowhere is there the slightest hint that they were somehow functioning outside their proper roles. The Assemblies of God, therefore, is correct when, in its official position paper on women, it declares:

> The instances of women filling leadership roles in the Bible should be taken as divinely approved pattern, not as exceptions to divine

decrees. Even a limited number of women with Scripturally commended leadership roles affirms that God does indeed call women to spiritual leadership.[65]

"But," some will ask, "what about Paul's call for female silence and submission in I Timothy 2:11-12 and I Corinthians 14:34-35?" The following points provide clear understanding of the situation.

- These passages should never be used, as they commonly are, as a canon within the canon concerning the status of women in the Church. The many passages that show women functioning in leadership should be given equal status with these two passages.
- The evidence is overwhelming that, in these two passages, Paul is addressing local, cultural situations that existed in Corinth and Ephesus. The passages are on the level of Paul's directives to believers to greet one another with a holy kiss and for women to wear a head covering when praying and prophesying—for cultural reasons—should they so choose.

These passages were not meant to be universal guidelines for church order and, in the process, for excluding women from leadership in the Church.[66]

---

[65] "The Role of Women in Ministry As Described in Holy Scripture: A Position Paper Adopted By the General Presbytery, August 1990," *Pentecostal Evangel* (Oct. 28, 1990): 12-15.

[66] For a thorough treatment of this issue see Susan Hyatt, *In the Spirit We're Equal* (Dallas: Hyatt Press, 1998).

CHARACTERISTIC 5:
Biblical Leadership Is Bible-Based and Spirit-Led.

Revival leaders, such as Wesley, Whitfield, Edwards, Finney, and others, were people of the Word, and they were also people who valued the dynamic and spontaneous working of the Holy Spirit in their midst. Historically, a sterile, institutionalized leadership has always quenched the Holy Spirit and, by the same token, revival.

To see Biblical revival in this generation, we must have leaders who value the powerful workings of the Holy Spirit in and through the people of God. Such leaders will not be slavishly bound to either ritual or pre-determined order, but will be open to—and even desire—the inbreaking of the Holy Spirit into their personal lives and into the meetings for which they have responsibility.

To be truly Spirit-led, however, the leader must be a person of the Word, because the Spirit and the Word work together. Being both radically open to the Spirit and totally committed to pursuing Biblical truth will provide a stability that will keep a revival on course and not allow it to crash on the rocks of religious extremes and fanaticism.

To "seek the Lord" does not mean we pray harder, louder, or longer. To "seek the Lord" means that we move from an approach to God that is centered in ourselves, with our own self-interests at the forefront, to an approach that is centered in Him, with His interests at the forefront of the relationship. We are no longer to relate to God on the basis of what He can do for us, but on the basis of how we can know Him and be more fully conformed to His character, will, and purpose.

Chapter 15

BEYOND REVIVAL:
SEEK THE LORD AND LIVE

⁴For thus says the Lord to the house of Israel: "Seek Me and live ⁵But do not seek Bethel, nor enter Gilgal, nor cross over to Beersheba; for Gilgal shall go into captivity, and Bethel shall come to nothing. ⁶Seek the Lord and live ...." – Amos 4:4-6

In 1976, Sue and I were conducting the first meeting of a new ministry and congregation that we were launching in Saint John, New Brunswick. During that gathering, God manifest His presence in an incredible way and revealed a truth to us that has become a guiding principle for our lives. We were meeting in a room at the YMCA, and Sue was speaking. The presence of God was manifest so powerfully that she had to grip the podium to keep from falling to the floor. At the same time, a prophetic word came forth based on Amos 5:4-6a.

⁴· *For thus says the Lord to the house of Israel:*

"Seek Me and live;
⁵· *But do not seek Bethel,*
Nor enter Gilgal,
Nor cross over to Beersheba;
For Gilgal shall go into captivity,
And Bethel shall come to nothing.

6. *Seek the Lord and live, …*

God was telling us not to study what someone else was doing in another city in order to try to duplicate it in Saint John. We were to seek Him through prayer and His Word, and we were to allow His work there to emerge out of our fellowship with Him. If we were to copy someone else's program or structure, what we did would be of temporal value. But if our work and ministry flowed out of our fellowship with Him in prayer and His Word, then what we did would last for eternity.

What It Means to "Seek the Lord"

To "seek the Lord" does not mean we pray harder, louder, or longer. To "seek the Lord" means that we move from an approach to God that is centered in ourselves, with our own self-interests at the forefront, to an approach that is centered in Him, with His interests at the forefront of the relationship. We are no longer to relate to God on the basis of what He can do for us, but on the basis of how we can know Him and be more fully conformed to His character, will, and purpose. The prayerful and diligent study of Scripture is, therefore, central in what it means to "seek the Lord."

In making my point, I am not suggesting that we should never ask God for anything. But as a matter of principal, we must change our attitude from one that is centered in "me, my needs and desires," to one that is centered in the Lord, His kingdom and His will. This means that we must spend much time in His Word and that our prayer times must be times of fellowship, praise, thanksgiving, and worship, rather than times of petitioning, commanding, or begging.

SUGGESTION 1:
Don't Seek the Gifts; Seek the Giver of the Gifts.

In the early 1950s, a certain pastor attended a William Branham crusade and was awed by the miraculous gifts that he saw demonstrated through Branham. The pastor returned home and announced to his wife and congregation that he was shutting himself away in his office to fast and pray until God gave him a ministry like Brother Branham (if he had known the error and deception into which Branham would fall, I am sure he would not have been so quick to seek a ministry like his). Anyway, this brother fasted for 84 days and died without hearing from God. What was the problem? He was not seeking the Lord. His fasting and praying were self-serving. He was seeking a ministry that he thought would give him increased prestige.

The Gospels clearly reveal that religious activities carried out from wrong motives are an abomination to God. This is borne out in the Gospel accounts of Jesus' encounters with the Pharisees. In spite of the fact that they prayed, fasted, and tithed, they were the recipients of Jesus' most severe rebukes because of their self-centered, self-serving motives.

This is also clear in the word of the Lord to Zechariah, concerning the people of Israel and their self-centered religious activities.

4. The LORD of Heaven's Armies sent me this message in reply: 5 "Say to all your people and your priests, 'During these seventy years of exile, when you fasted and mourned in the summer and in early autumn, was it really for me that you were fasting? 6 And even now in your holy festivals, aren't you eating and drinking just to please yourselves?
(Zechariah 7:4-6; New Living Translation)

SUGGESTION 2:
Don't Seek Healing; Seek the Healer.

When I was three weeks old, my seven-year-old brother, nicknamed Pete, was run over by a large, farm tractor that had a planter with plows attached to it. My parents rushed him, unconscious and with blood bubbling from his eyes, nose, mouth and ears, to the nearest hospital where he was examined by three physicians. They determined that, in addition to whatever other injuries he may have had, he had at least one broken rib puncturing a lung, and they agreed that he would not live more than ten minutes.

The only thing on my Dad's mind at this time was that, for five years, he had ignored a call from God to full-time ministry. With only a fourth grade education and the responsibility of a young family to care for, he felt that full-time ministry was impossible. He had told no one of God's dealings.

Now, faced with the possible death of his son, he stepped into a restroom, raised his right hand and prayed a three-word prayer: "Lord, I'm ready!" It was a prayer of surrender. It was a prayer in which

God's interests were placed above all others, including his own.

Suddenly, the gift of faith dropped into his heart and he knew that Pete was going to be okay. He didn't know how he knew, but he knew. After about an hour, one of the doctors returned to the waiting room and said,

Mr. Hyatt, there has been a Higher Power here tonight. We know that your son had a broken rib puncturing one of his lungs. But we have completed the x-rays, and he doesn't have a broken bone in his body, and the bleeding has stopped.

My brother, Pete, is well and healthy today. How did this miracle happen? I believe it had to do with my Dad putting God's interests ahead of his own. Think about it! He did not pray for healing. Nor did he rebuke the devil. He did not call an intercessory prayer group or a healing evangelist. Instead, he responded in simple faith to something God had been asking of him for some time. He cut through all of the excuses and bowed before God. God's interests totally filled his heart and mind, and God's power was manifest in an amazing way. Despite the doctors' prognosis, Pete was instantly healed.

I am convinced that we do not see greater miracles of healing today because we tend to be more preoccupied with healing than we are with the Healer. If we will put the interests of the Healer ahead of our own interests, I believe that God's healing power will be mightily revealed in our midst—and we may yet see another "healing revival."

SUGGESTION 3:

Don't Seek Provision; Seek the Provider.

All Saints Anglican Church in Sunderland, England took on an extensive building project around 1900. Because of some unexpected challenges, they found themselves burdened with a financial debt they were unable to pay. About this time, the church's rector, A. A. Boddy, heard about the Azusa Street Revival in America. The news stirred an intense desire in his heart for God, and consequently, he and many of his parishioners began to seek God diligently. A powerful revival broke out in their midst, and All Saints became a great center of revival.

As word spread, the curious and hungry traveled to Sunderland from throughout the United Kingdom and Europe. Well-known Pentecostal evangelist, Smith Wigglesworth, traveled to All Saints in 1907 and was baptized in the Holy Spirit when Mrs. Boddy, the pastor's wife, laid hands on him. But much more than this happened!

In the midst of seeking God and experiencing His presence and power, Pastor Boddy and the people of All Saints almost forgot about the financial debt. Nevertheless, in the midst of the revival, without any fundraising efforts on their part, all the money to pay the dept was given. They were so impressed that they inscribed the following statement on the cornerstone of their building:

The fire fell and burned up the debt.

The miracle of provision happened when they stopped seeking money and began to seek God. Their need was supplied, and the words of the Psalmist rang true:

The young lions do lack and suffer hunger,
but they that seek the Lord shall not lack any
good thing (Psalm 34:10).

Those who stand on the Promises of God have heard about the transference of worldly wealth into the hands of believers, according to Proverbs 13:22. Although we serve a merciful and forgiving God, there is reason to question whether this promise will be fulfilled for a generation that is seeking money. But it is surely a promise of God to those who seek Him.

SUGGESTION 4:
Don't Seek Revival; Seek the God of Revival.

I had the privilege of writing the official book for the Azusa Street Centennial Celebration that convened in Los Angeles in 2006 with an attendance of over 50,000 people from around the world. In doing the research for this book, entitled *Fire on the Earth*, I reread the original documents from the revival.

As I read, I was struck by the fact that William Seymour and other leaders at Azusa Street were not seeking revival. They were seeking God. Seymour tells how, even before he met Charles Parham in Houston, his heart was so hungry "to have more of God." He was not hungry to have a big ministry. He was not hungry to pastor a big church. He was not hungry to lead a great revival. He was hungry "to have more of God." He and others were seeking God, and God sent an earth-shaking, global revival.

In his *Lectures on Revival*, Charles Finney tells of the many invitations he had received from churches and pastors wanting him to travel to their communities to promote revival. This was his conclusion:

> When I came to weigh their reasons, I have sometimes found every one of them to be selfish. And God would look upon every one with abhorrence.[67]

Some wanted revival in order to raise their social status and influence. Others wanted revival to increase the numbers attending their meetings, which in turn would enable them to build new and larger buildings. Still others wanted revival so that they would feel superior to one or more congregations with whom they felt a sense of competition. They were not seeking the Lord. They were seeking revival, and that from self-centered motives. Finney rightfully refused their requests.

Conclusion

God is merciful, but motives still matter. At some point, the Spirit comes, not to confirm that we are already perfect, but to convict, to comfort, to guide us into all truth, and to glorify Jesus (John 16:5-15).

---

[67] Charles G. Finney, *Revival Lectures* (Grand Rapids: Fleming H. Revell, n.d.), 351.

And He does this as we seek Him.

God works with us to help correct our motives for wanting revival. We love Him because He first loved us (1 John 4:19), and yet He comes to us in a special way that we call "revival" when we truly turn from self to Him. We surrender our personal agendas to Him, and He imparts to us His agenda, which is far better. Where does revival start? In the heart of God! And as we seek Him, and not revival *per se*, He pours out His Spirit in what we call "revival."

As we truly seek Him, making His priorities our priorities and His interests our interests, there will come a rest and peace in our souls such as we have not known. We become consumed with His desires and His business, and suddenly we find that He is looking after our desires and our business in ways we could never have imagined. This is what Jesus was talking about when He said:

> But seek first the kingdom of God and His righteousness, and all these things will be added to you (Matthew 6:33).

In this place of desiring Him and His ways above all else, we will find that our spirit has been sensitized to discern between what is of God and what is not of God. And in the midst of *Revival Fire*, we will be better able to flow with the Holy Spirit and to discern between the true and the false.

ABOUT THE AUTHOR

Dr. Eddie L. Hyatt teaches with a unique blend of Holy Spirit anointing, Biblical and historical acumen, academic excellence, and almost 40 years of ministry experience. His theme is "Spiritual Awakening and Biblical Thinking," with the motive that God and *His* ways and means will be known. His ministry touches both "the head and the heart."

He earned his Doctor of Ministry degree from Regent University, his Master of Divinity and Master of Arts degrees from Oral Roberts University. A graduate of both Southwestern University and Christ for the Nations Institute, he also studied at Fuller Theological Seminary.

Eddie has lectured on Revival, Church History and various Biblical themes in churches, conferences, and educational institutions, including Oxford University, Oral Roberts University, Zion Bible Institute and Christ for the Nations Institute. He was on the ministry team at the Azusa Street Centennial Celebration in Los Angeles in 2006, for which he was also commissioned to write the two official books. He also was part of the ministry team for the Azusa Asia-Indonesia Celebrations in Jakarta, Indonesia, the same year. He has authored several books, the most popular of which is *2000 Years of Charismatic Christianity*.

Eddie and his wife, Dr. Susan Hyatt, reside in Tulsa Oklahoma. In addition to writing, teaching, and traveling, they are establishing the Int'l Christian Women's Hall of Fame and the Christian Historical Society of Canada, Inc.

CONTACT INFORMATION
Eddie L. Hyatt
Hyatt Int'l Ministries
9933 S. 108th East Ave. • Tulsa, OK 74133
www.eddiehyatt.com   dreddiehyatt@gmail.com

OTHER BOOKS by DR EDDIE L. HYATT

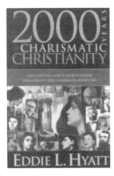

These books are available at local Christian bookstores,
www.amazon.com and www.eddiehyatt.com/bookstore.html

BOOKS by DR. SUSAN C. HYATT

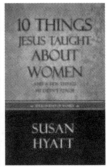

These and other publications are available from the author:
DrSueHyatt@live.com and www.icwhp.org/bookstore.html

Visit www.icwhp.org for a free course and information
about the Int'l Christian Women's Hall of Fame.

To Order Additional Copies Of
REVIVAL FIRE

go to www.EddieHyatt.com and click Bookstore
or Email DrEddieHyatt@gmail.com.
Bulk discounts are available.

The author is available to teach and minister on this and other important topics.

Eddie Hyatt is issuing a serious warning to all of us in the revival movement to stay close to Jesus and the B-I-B-L-E. When I read it, I felt comforted and challenged. When you are looking at a new movement, it is the love of the truth, not naïveté, which helps you find what the Lord wants you to learn and experience in it. It is a highly informative and interesting read. Eddie is not a detractor; he's one of us, and he's got a message we need to hear. Let's take our medicine and receive it in love.

> MELINDA FISH
> Author and Revivalist, River City Church of Pittsburgh, Trafford, PA

Let me say how much I enjoyed reading this book, how better I know you now through its pages, and how deeply I appreciate you, the breadth and depth of your scholarship, and the passion you have for the word of God and the power of the Holy Spirit. You are a breath of fresh air, biblically and theologically. Your insights, critique, correction, and biblical and practical prescriptions of much that is falsely called Christian and Charismatic today are welcome. Believe me, I can trust just about anything you write because of the balance you bring.

> TREVOR GRIZZLE, PH.D.
> Senior Pastor and Professor, Oral Roberts University, Tulsa, OK

What a blessing the Lord has given us through you and Sue. I have taught the Word for thirty-five years and I am doubly blessed by your instructions because I know you teach the absolute Word of God. Thank you for the years you have continued to be faithful to His Word, and how you give it to us in such a simple yet profound way. I also thank the Lord for the way you and Sue continue to walk in integrity and love of the Lord.

> VALARIE OWEN
> Author and Bible Teacher, Irving, TX

This book is full of inspirational information that is written in a way that will connect you with a heritage of faith and power so you will "lift up your eyes from the place where you now stand" and run *your* course with adrenaline in your souls! Thank you, Eddie Hyatt, for a superb book.

> CINDY DUVAL AND LOIS & RAY TAUCHER
> Shekinah Glory Ministries, Tulsa, OK